Table of Contents – CONSTRUCT 3 Game Creation 2024

Preface

CONSTRUCT had revolutionized the world of 2D game creation, by providing easy drag-and-drop kind of interface for producing complex game logic, all without writing codes and scripts.

The goal of this book is to provide starters with rich technical information so the best decision and judgment can be exercised when creating 2D and 3D games through the cloud based CONSTRUCT 3. Construct Classic and CONSTRUCT2 are local Windows software which are considered as legacy and are not going to be covered in this book.

Throughout this book we will simply refer to CONSTRUCT 3 as C3. Earlier Construct versions are being referred to as C2. The latest C3 release as of the time of this writing is R407.

This is not a step-by-step tutorial. This is also not a guide book kind of overview material. We place our focus on the practical side of game creation – practical tips and techniques one will definitely need when starting out a 2D/3D game project. We also tell exactly what can and cannot be done with C3, and the kind of performance drawback that can be foreseen when the platform is not fed with the right inputs.

So, are you ready for the challenge?

Basic Concepts

What kinds of game are C3 optimized for? Is C3 3D capable?

C3 is a development platform that can be used to create a wide range of 2D games and applications. Its newer features also allow the creation of certain 3D games. C3 is NOT optimized for any particular game type but is more "general-purpose" oriented.

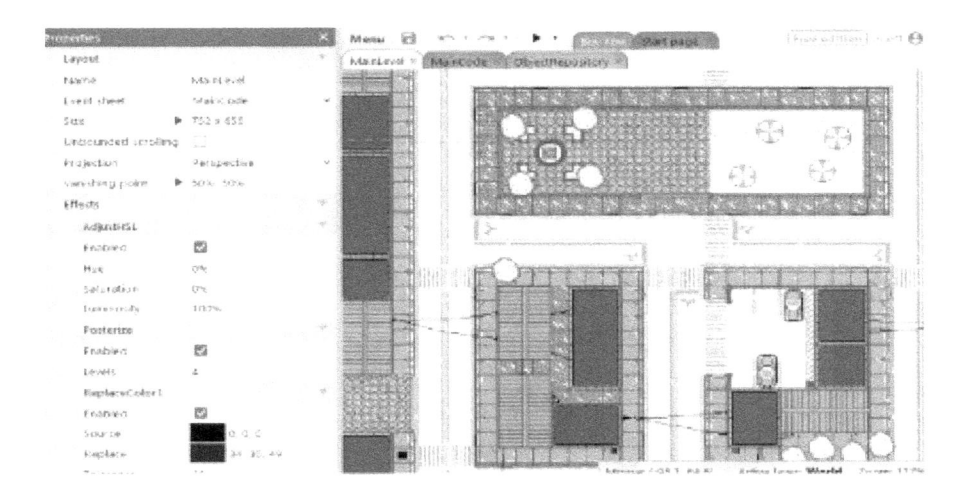

While Construct 3 isn't as advanced in 3D as engines like Unity or Unreal Engine, its 3D capabilities have been gradually evolving, providing tools for more-than-simple 3D effects and gameplay. Simply put, if you want to create a full blown 3D action shooter with a massive 3D world, shop somewhere else. C3 manipulates objects primarily as bitmaps in 2D mode. It does have the muscles for processing polygons the 3D style.

A unique feature of Construct 3's 3D support is its ability to combine 2D gameplay with 3D elements. This means developers can use traditional 2D sprites and layers, but incorporate 3D shapes, environments, or camera movements to create hybrid games that blend both 2D and 3D aspects.

Is C3 64 bit?

C3 is cloud based and can be run on web browsers. You can run it on 32 bit or 64 bit OS. It has a subscription model so you can pay on a monthly or yearly basis. A free trial version is available.

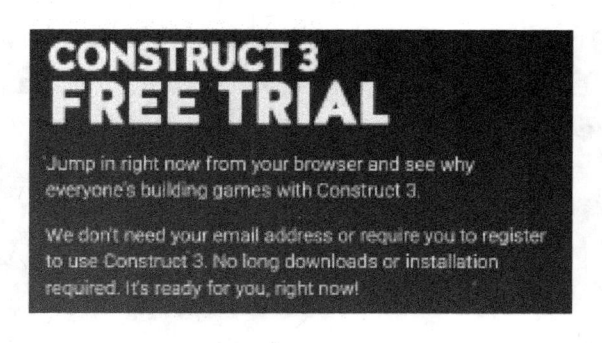

You can try it out as a guest. Or you can register for a free account and get more resources:

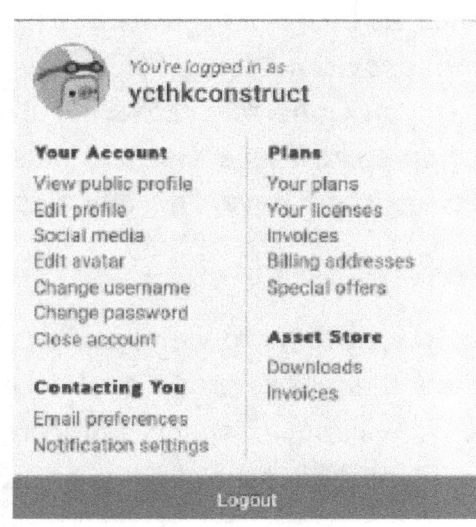

Why is C3 a good choice for elementary game creation?

First of all, the C3 user interface (UI) is one of the best I have ever seen in terms of ease of use and flexibility. It is MUCH MUCH better than the Director/Flash interface. It does not need any scripting (it does support scripting). The arrangement of the interface functions and objects are very logical, making things very easy to understand.

You can think of C3 as a visual scripting platform. Instead of writing scripts yourself, C3 gives you visual menus and forms so you can pick up choices via drag and drop and formulate scripts without writing codes. C3 then generates the necessary scripts and commands for you transparently in the background.

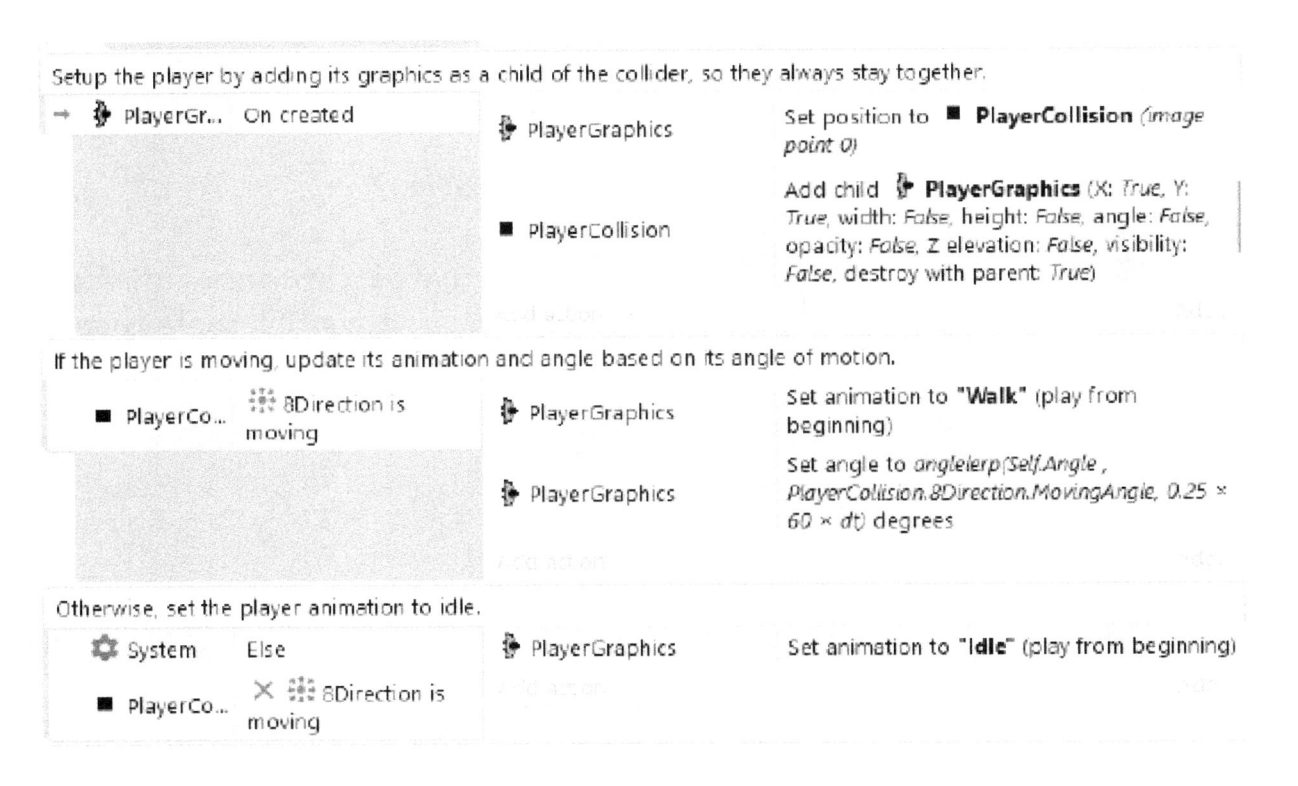

C3 further allows you to create games that run on platforms other than PC. In fact, C3 builds HTML5 games which can run on most platforms that support web browsing. You can even run C3 on a mobile phone (you can choose between desktop UI and mobile UI), and in different languages.

Is C3 a good choice for advanced level game creation?

Based on my experience with the C3 UI and the actual performance outcome, I am comfortable to tell you that certain types of game can be professionally created with C3:

- the Candy Crush type of puzzle game
- the Mario Brothers type of 2D action game
- the R-Type/1942 kind of shooting game
- the YS kind of RPG game
- any bird-eye view type of action game

One good thing about C3 is that it is a quite stable platform, that unknown weird runtime errors are not common at all. Do note that C3 does not offer very rich functions for graphic and special effect preparation by itself. The graphic editor that comes with it is pretty basic.

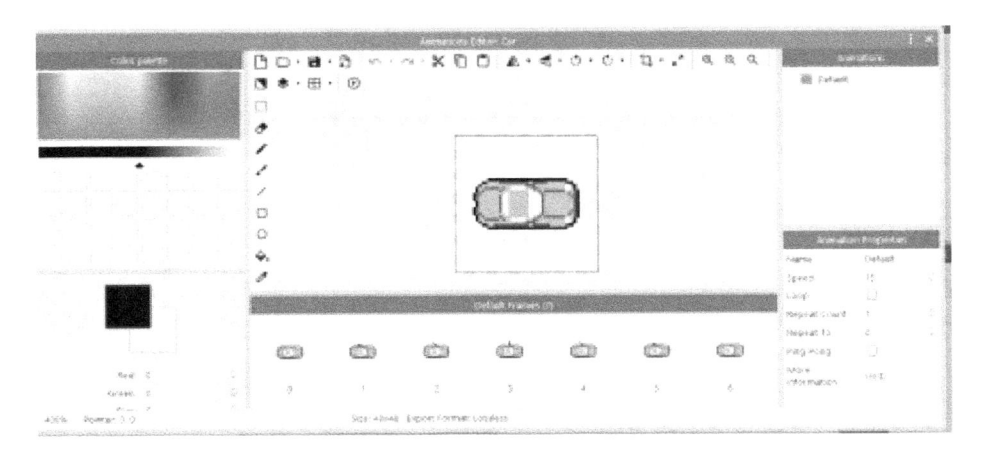

You may want to come up with your own artworks and music using other tools, then import them into C3. Or you may use the new Construct Animate software (we will talk about this software later).

C3 does provide templates to start with, making it easy to create games:

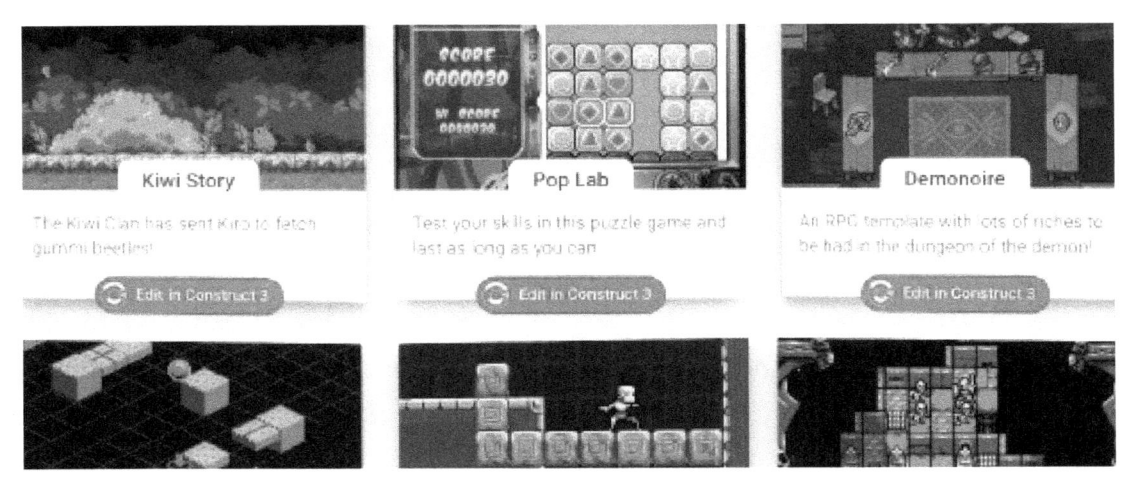

Do I need any special licenses for game creation?

For a free trial you do NOT need to register for an account first. HOWEVER, with an account you will have less limitations.

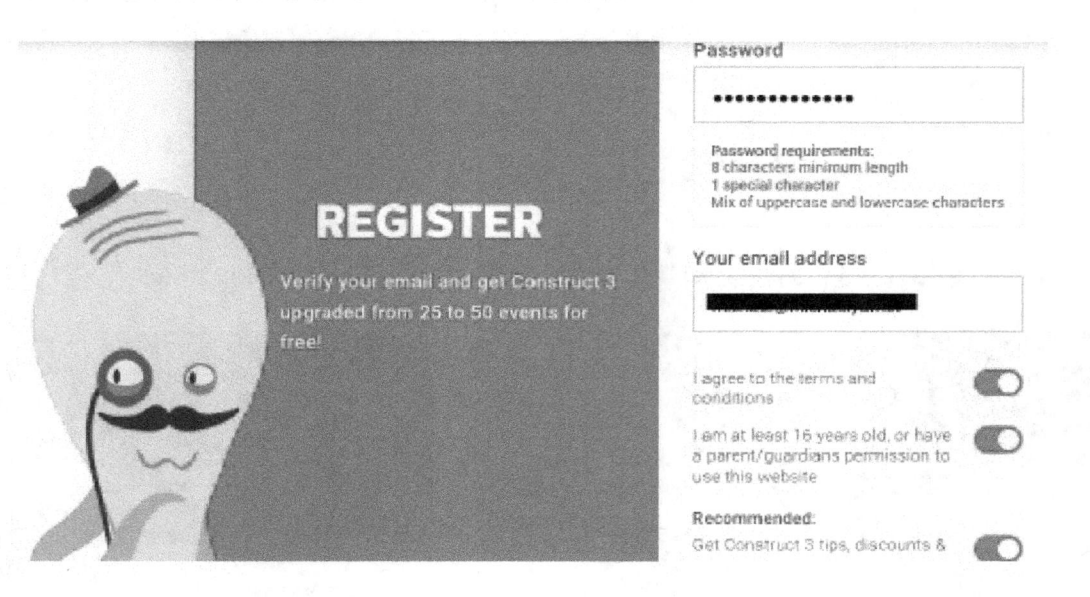

C3 has several licensing modes. If you are not planning to make a profit, the free trial license is good enough. To sell games for profit you need to have an individual license if you are a single user startup, or a business license which requires that you specify the number of seats required. There is also an educational license for training school and the like. In any case you do not need to pay any royalties for selling your creation.

The FREE trial has quite many limitations. For example, you cannot have unlimited events per event sheet:

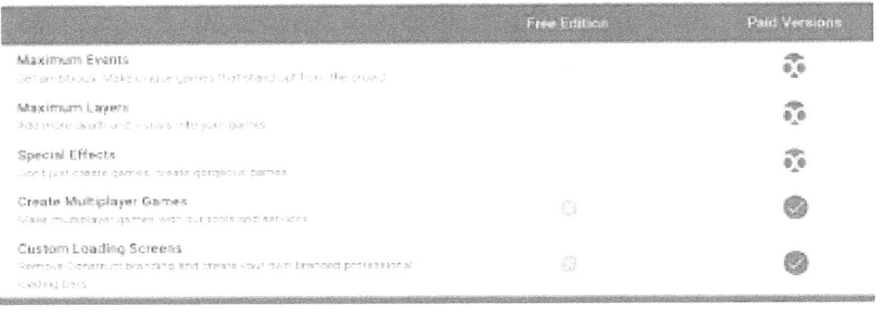

The free edition has limitations but is still good for you to try out the various features.

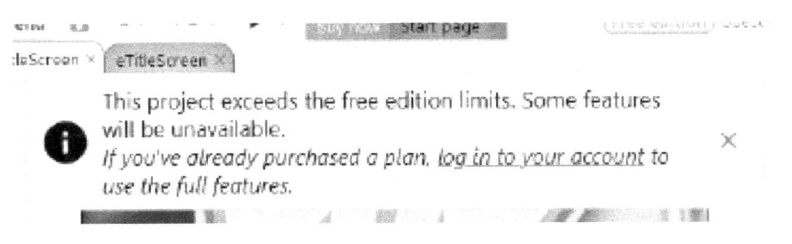

Is C3 going to be easy (for me) if I have rich background in procedural programming languages like C and Pascal?

It is hard to say. The thing is, the C3 engine is an event driven system, which is NOT procedural at all. It is not just about difference in language syntax. It is a totally different way of thinking. Procedural thinking is usually top-down, with heavy focus on procedures and functions. An event driven system, on the other hand, consists of objects with different behaviors and properties, all interacting via events (which in turn would trigger actions).

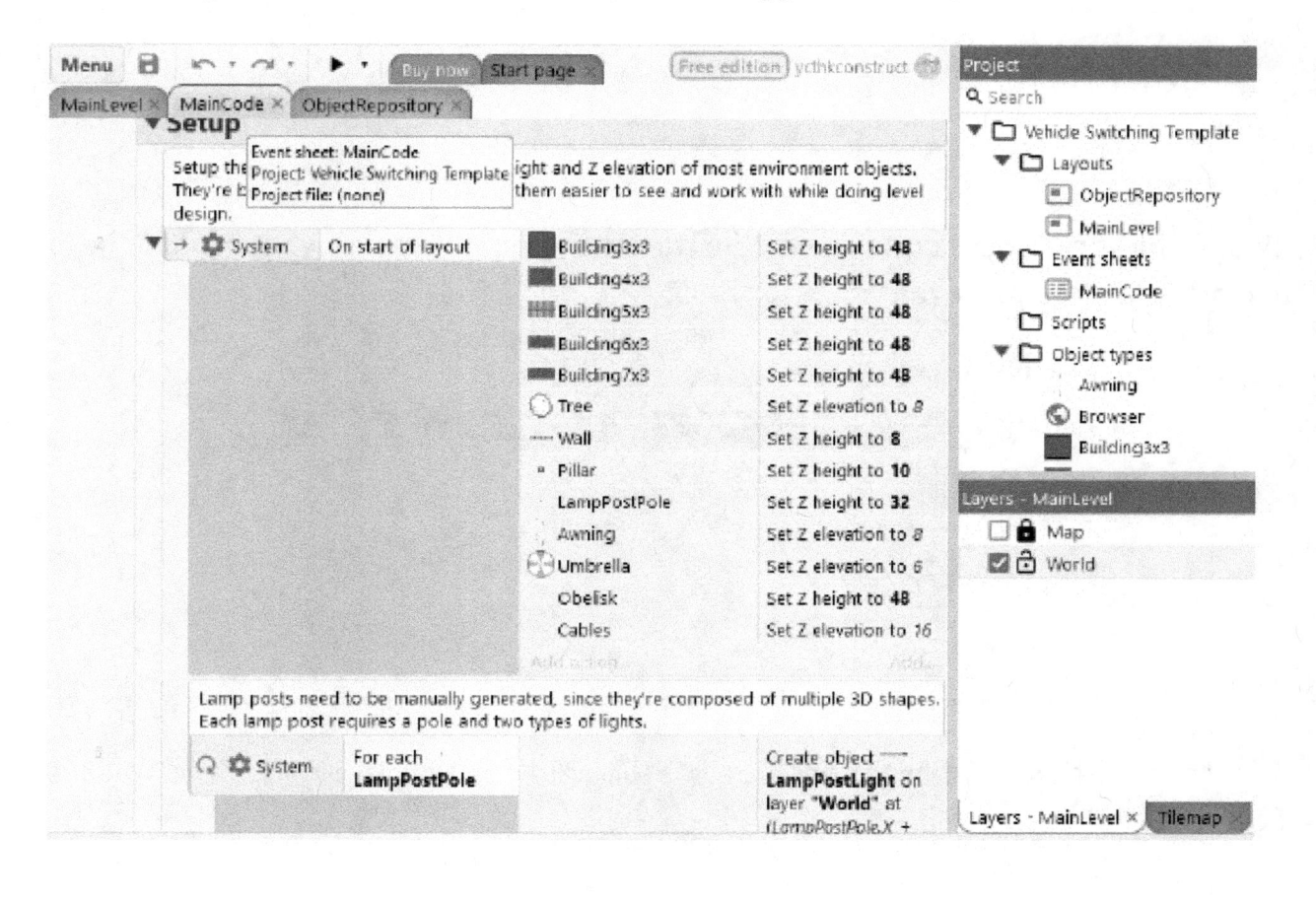

Why would one prefer C3 over GM Studio for game creation?

Game Maker GM Studio offers the Game Maker Language (GML) for scripting purpose. GML is sort of a scripting language that works and looks like something in between Pascal and C. GML is easier to learn than a true Object Oriented Language such as C++. At the same time it allows flexibility in coding. **To truly utilize the power of GM Studio one will for sure need to code.**

In contrast, C3 's interactive interface is so powerful that the need for coding is minimal. C3 does support scripting, but you shouldn't need to script much. Its major selling point is no-programming!

Why would one prefer C3 over GDevelop for game creation?

The two are in fact highly similar in functionalities. Both of them are very powerful and easy to use.

C3 is cloud based only and requires licensing. GDevelop can be run online or locally and has a completely free version with relatively few limitations.

Why would one prefer C3 over Clickteam Fusion for game creation?

C3 is highly similar to Clickteam Fusion in the way games can be built (so are the concepts behind their event driven mechanisms). C3 can export projects to a wide variety of platforms, although HTML5 is the main stream.

C3 is cloud based so that local installation is not required. You pay license fee on a monthly/yearly basis. Fusion requires installation locally and you do not have to pay any license fee. However, Fusion development seems to be slow (haven't seen version 3 for years).

Is C3 compatible with C2?

CAPX file created by C2 can be opened through Menu – Open - Open Local file. Compatibility really depends on the features used in the project.

The way things work are almost identical. If you are good at C2 then you should have no problem using C3, Conversion is automatic.

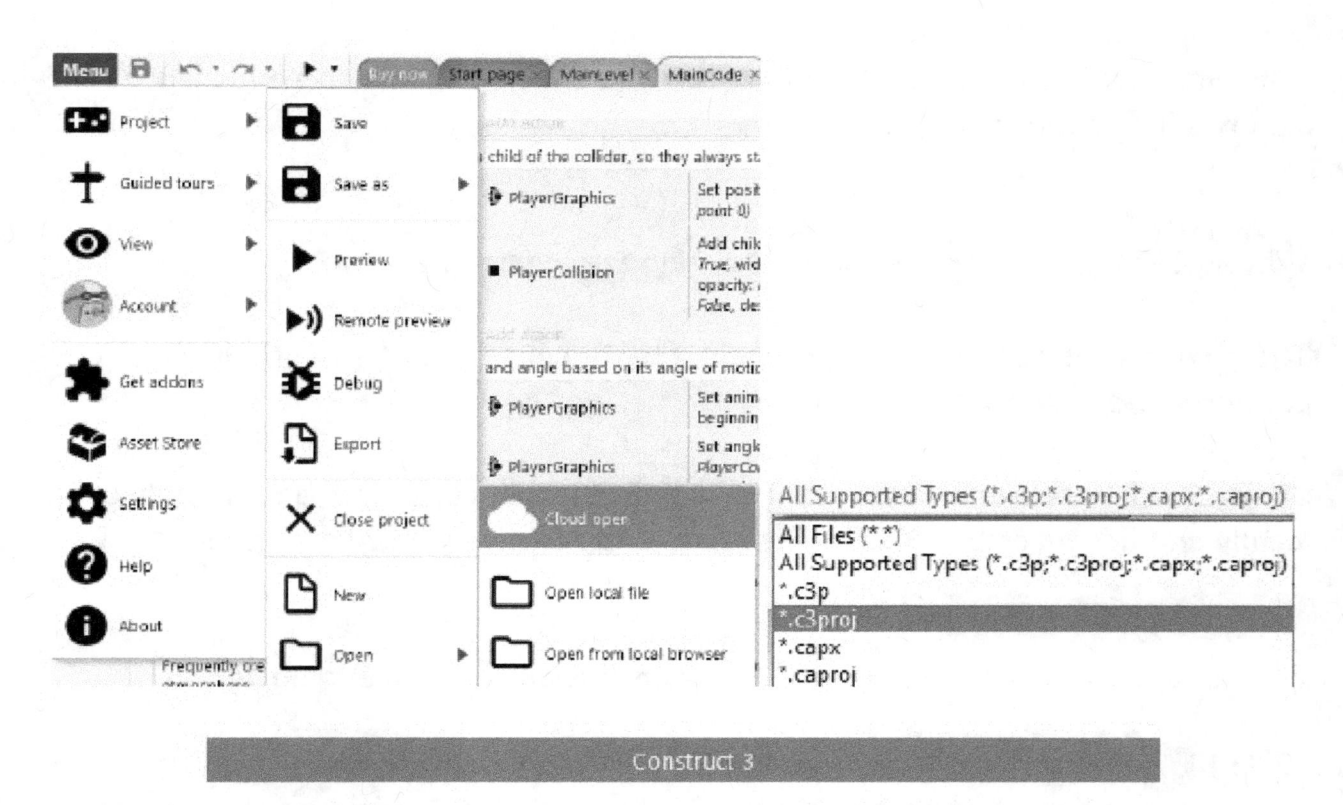

Currently, files saved to browser storage may be deleted by the browser under certain circumstances. Would you like to enable persistent storage? This should ensure the browser does not delete files automatically. **Note:** we strongly recommend also keeping regular backups while using this save option to avoid accidental data loss.

What is the difference between local file and local browser?

Local file is file stored in the local file system. Local browser refers to browser storage (and possibly cache) in the local drive. Some web browsers clean up such storage automatically and periodically so I would not recommend that you use this option.

Can I master C3 without understanding any programming concept?

Frankly, no. Even though C3 works as a visual tool, its core is no different from a traditional object oriented development system. It is fully event driven, and the only difference is that you may define the various event conditions and actions via a graphical/menu based interface.

Almost all C3 objects that are shown on screen moving around and playing some sort of actions are sprites. Their interaction forms your game.

To effectively plan how these different sprite objects (and other object types) may interact, you'll need to fully understand the event-driven concept.

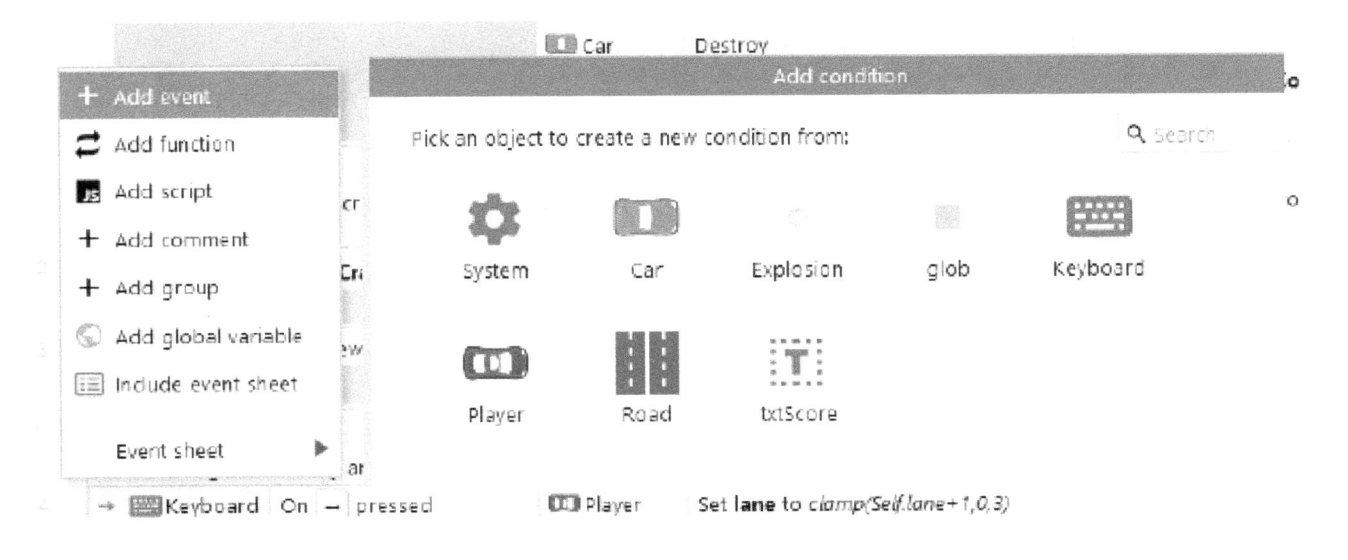

Can I make a game without a layout or an event sheet?

You need to know that whenever you create a game there must be at least one layout! And when you create such layout C3 will give you an empty event sheet automatically.

This is an empty event sheet

To start adding events, click **Add event** in the top-left corner of this view. You can also double-click or double-tap in a space. Alternatively you can bring up a menu by right-click or tap-and-hold or clicking the **Add...** link in the top-right.

Events are run from top-to-bottom once per tick (i.e. at the framerate), typically 60 times a second. An example event is shown below. The *conditions* are on the left and the *actions* are on the right. The actions only run when the conditions are met. The margin can be used to select or modify the whole event. For more information see How events work.

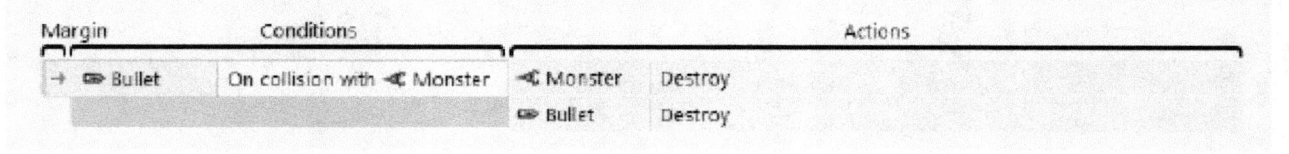

It is NOT a MUST for a layout to have an event sheet, as you can always right click and delete the event sheet. HOWEVER, without an event sheet your game is just not a game since there is no program in it at all.

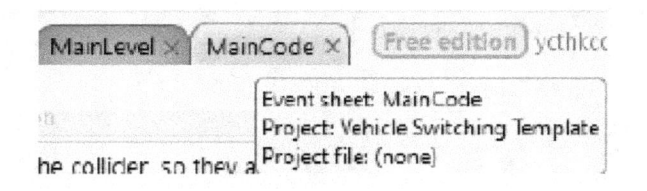

What is special about an event driven system? How does it work?

In an event driven environment, a program is structured in terms of events, with no preordered flow of control. Things do NOT start and proceed step by step. Instead, actions are associated with events, which will get invoked only when the corresponding event conditions are met (i.e. the event occurs). You do not know when these events will take place at design time. For example, object A has an action of shooting. This shooting action will not start UNLESS object B has an explosion. Whether or not object B will explode depends on whether the player can accurately hit object B with a missile object. Movement of the missile object is an action. The resulting collision (with object B) is an event. This event can trigger two sets of action: object B explodes and object A shoots.

In C3, an event can trigger multiple actions. For an event to "take place", you can even specify multiple conditions. Just keep in mind, you always define the conditions first prior to defining the actions.

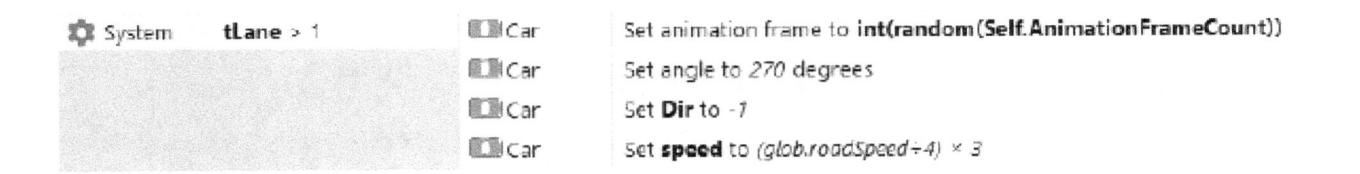

System	tLane > 1	Car	Set animation frame to int(random(Self.AnimationFrameCount))
		Car	Set angle to 270 degrees
		Car	Set **Dir** to -1
		Car	Set **speed** to (glob.roadSpeed÷4) × 3

C3 is event driven. It is also object oriented. Every item that shows up in the game is an object. Every object has a set of properties which represent the object's unique characteristics. They can be predefined, and some may even be manipulated at runtime through event triggered actions.

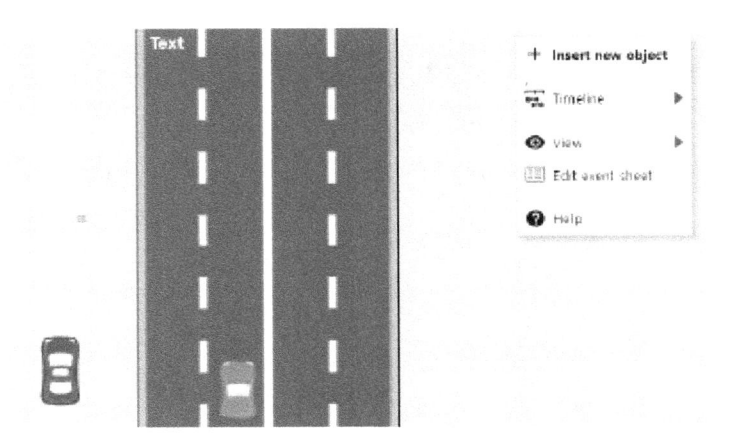

You can right click on the layout and choose Edit event sheet to invoke the Event Sheet. At the bottom of the event sheet you can click on Add Event to start writing a new event and its rules/actions.

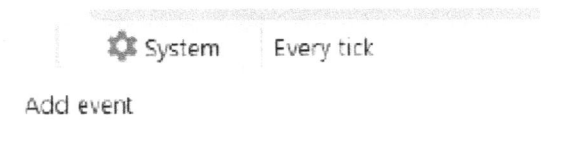

Then you pick an object for testing a condition:

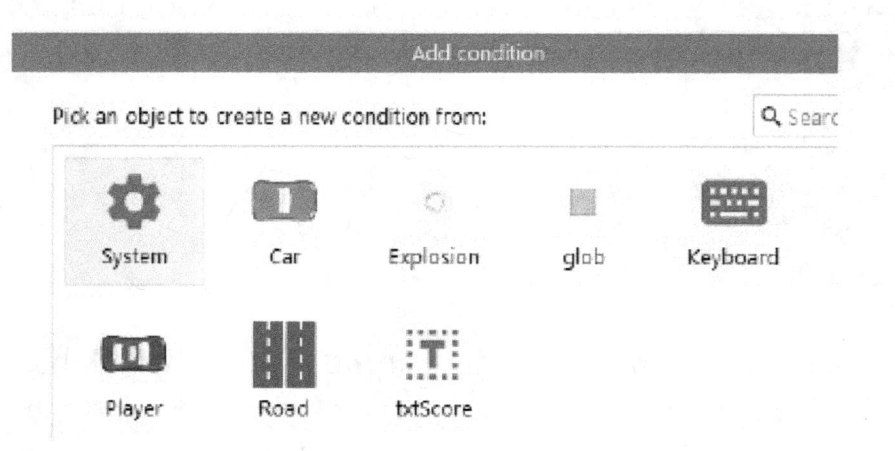

Then you pick a relevant event condition from the list:

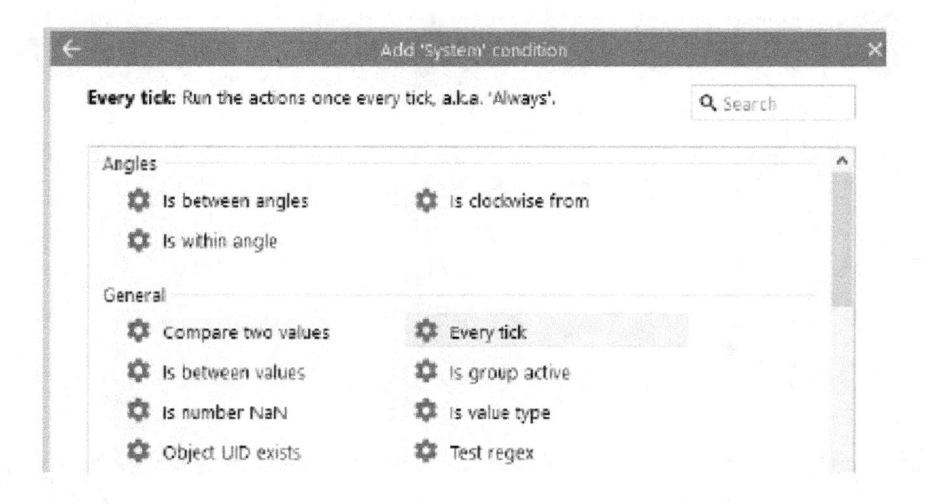

Then you define a logical comparison if needed:

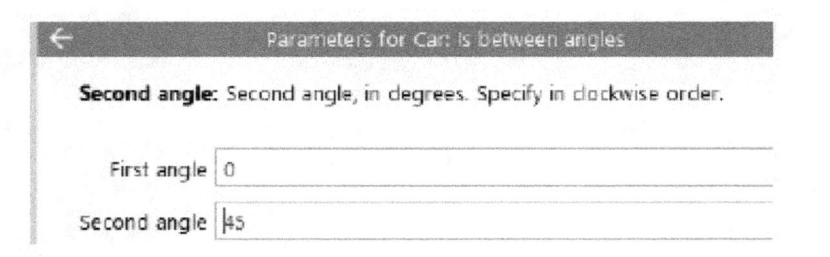

Then you click Add action to pick an object for carrying about an action:

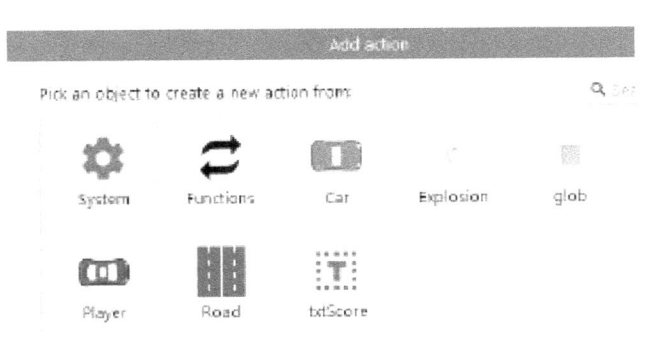

Then you pick the desired action and set the relevant value as needed, and add other actions if necessary.

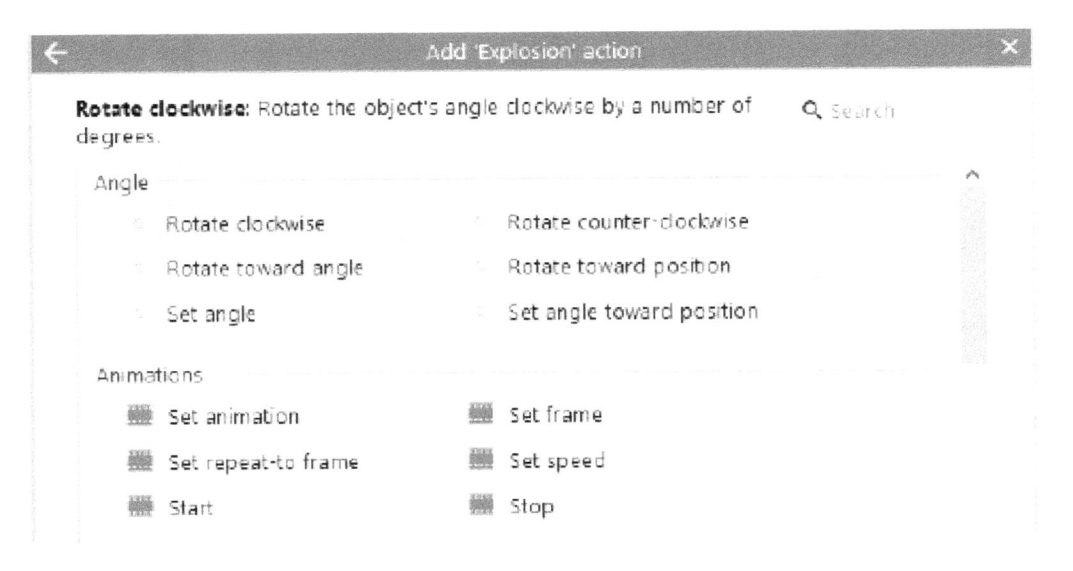

The resulting event sheet shows all the rules you have defined for the layout. Each layout can be associated with one event sheet.

Can I write script and use it in C3?

As an advanced option, yes. You can write Javascript. Right click on the Event

Sheet and choose Add Script, then you can write script on it directly.

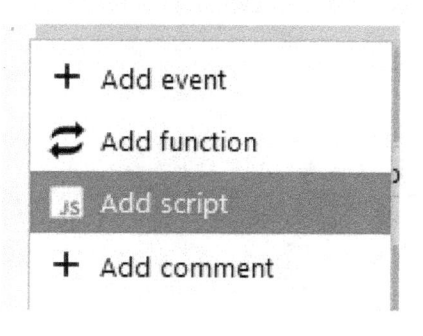

Separating graphic design from game design...

Through the C3 picture editor you can import graphics for further processing. You can load an image into it, or simply copy and paste from another paint program.

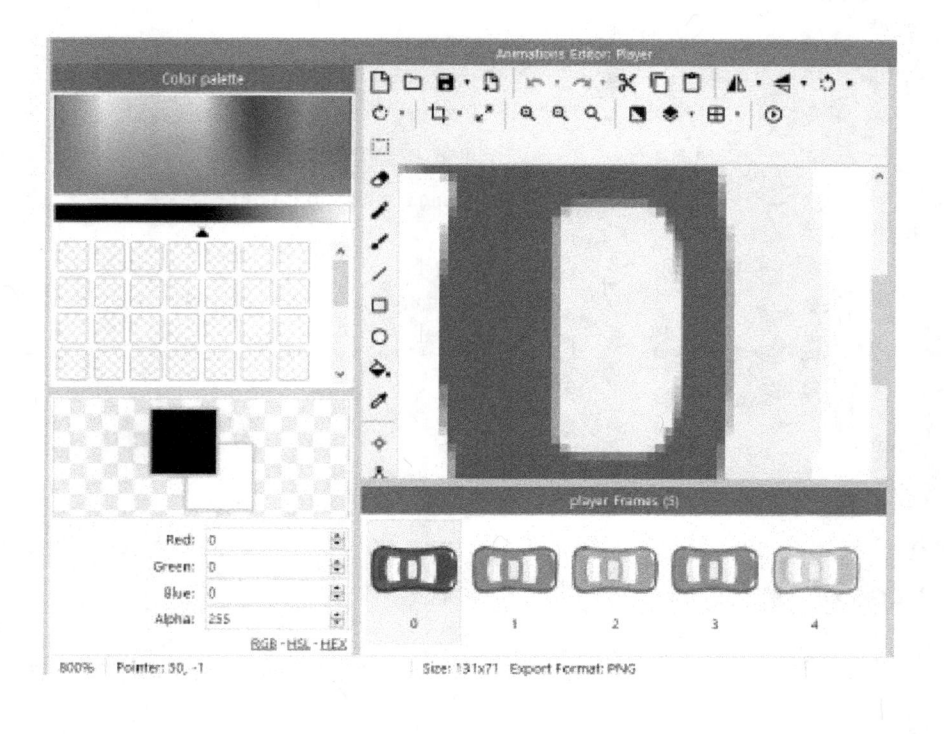

Graphic design is a very time consuming process. For an animation to look good you need as many frames as possible. And you need to create animations for different situations in different directions. That means there are MANY frames to create.

Once you are into the graphic and animation work, the entire game creation process will slow down. A common problem is for the programming team to wait for finished artworks and animations from the media team prior to putting things together. Assuming what you have got is a small team, I would suggest that you clearly break down the game creation process into two sub-processes, with one focusing on the logical "programming" side and another on media (graphics, animation, sound effects...etc) development.

During level design, the programming guy does not really have to use "real stuff". Object actions and events can be designed and implemented through using simple symbolic artworks. For example, instead of waiting for the media design guy to get you a finished Jet you can use a basic plane-like artwork for configuring all the relevant properties, events and actions first.

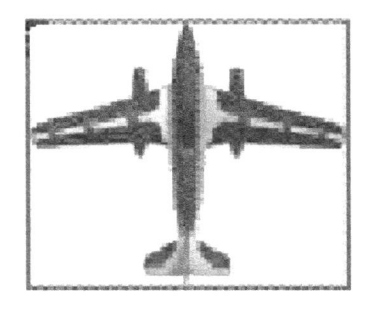 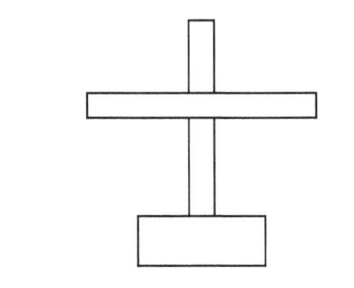

Once the programming works are done and fully tested you may slowly import and "fit in" the real stuff.

For your information, the graphic design guy would need to prepare and implement different animation sequences for the object. The actual use of these sequences is usually determined by the programming guy, through logic implemented in the event mechanisms.

As previously said, you can always prepare graphics via another paint program, then "export" to the C3 picture editor through COPY and PASTE OR SAVE and OPEN as long as the pictures are in JPG, JPEG, GIF, SVG or PNG format.

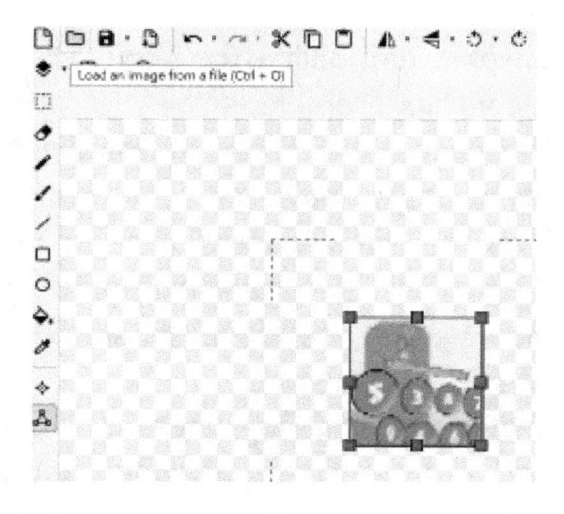

Sometimes copy and paste may give no result on some windows desktop. Tjhen you will need the help of a clipboard manager utility to do the pasting.

You can later export the image as PNG or JPEG files (it is always good to backup your resources locally):

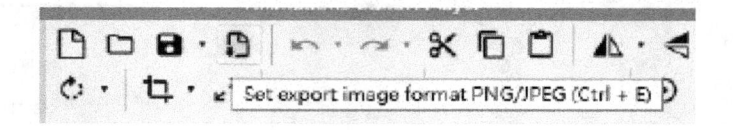

Very importantly, you can fine tune the image point and the collision polygon of an object via the picture editor in C3:

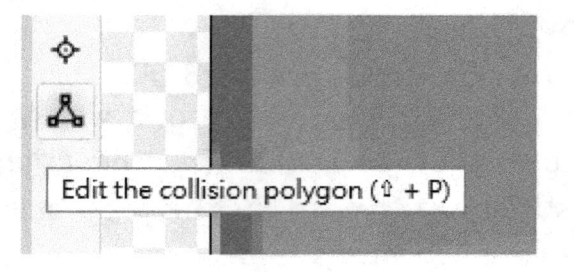

By default there is already a collision polygon "guessed" by the program so you do not need to make a custom one, UNLESS the default one is not up to your satisfaction. Also note that background tile does not use collision polygon at all.

You can drag and points to adjust the polygon, or right click and ask C3 to "guess" again. And you can choose to apply it to all the frames of the animation.

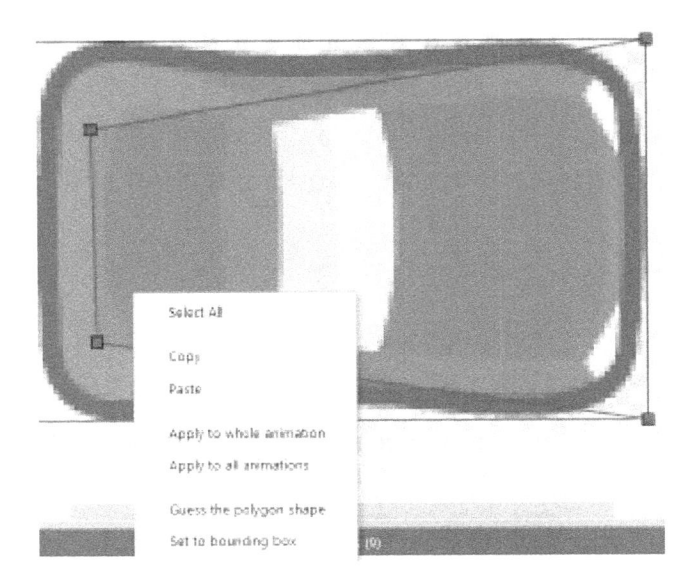

Why is it important to set the image point correctly?

The image point is NOT for collision checking. It is for determining the location of the sprite. If your image point is not at the center of the sprite, you may not be able to position the sprite accurately.

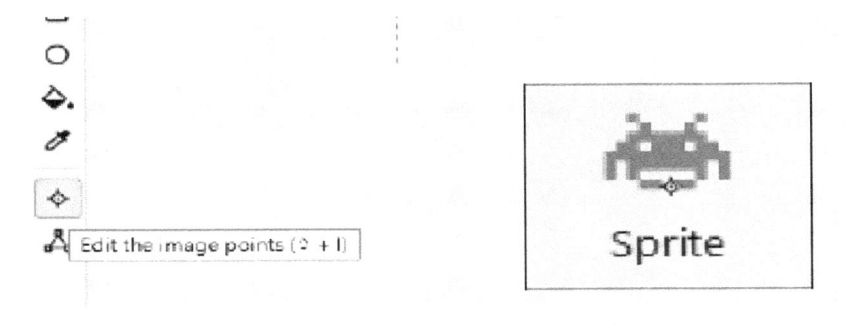

I am confused – how do the terms Application, Game, Layout, and Window relate to each others?

In the context of CONSTRUCT game creation:
- an application represents a game
- a layout holds a game level
- an application shows up on your desktop through its window
- each application should have only one window
- each application can have one or more layouts
- each layout can belong to only one application
- each project holds one and only one application

When you create a new program in C3, you can choose to save on the cloud if your browser allows popup window:

Or you can download a local copy (in c3p format):

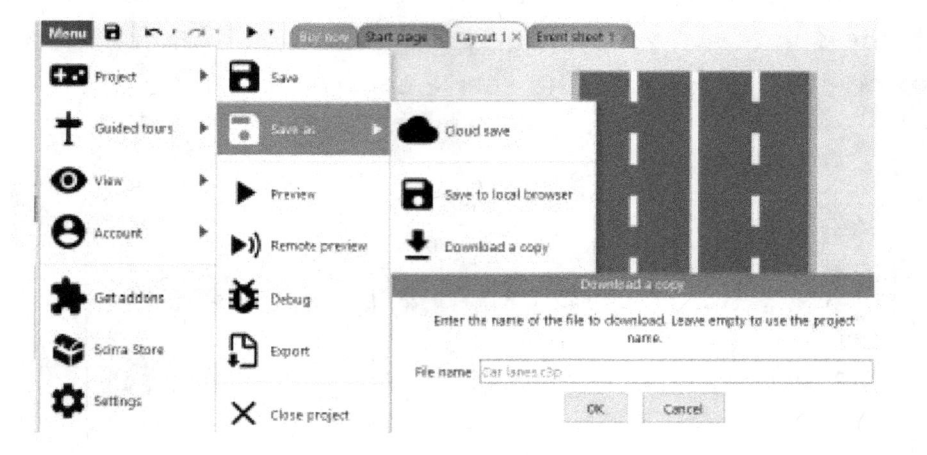

What is the relationship between a viewport, a layout and a layer?

On a Windows desktop, all applications exist in the form of a "window". In the previous version of Construct, a window displays a layout. A layout contains a game level. You may think of a window as a view port for viewing a layout (and the game level presented by the layout). Since C3, the term viewport is formally used in place of "window" due to the popularity of non-window targets.

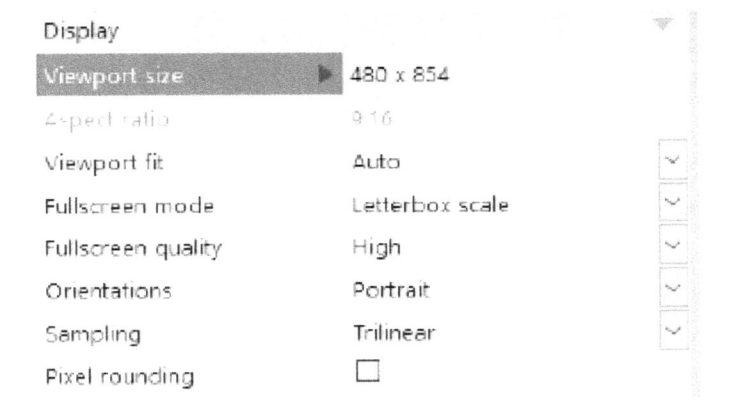

Each layout can have multiple layers. Layers is a design time feature which allows you to easily arrange the level objects. Put it this way, a flat layout means there is only one layer. When multiple layers are involved, you need to determine how your objects are to be placed (for example, all background objects at one layer and other active objects on another layer). There is no strict rule to follow – arrangement is entirely up to you.

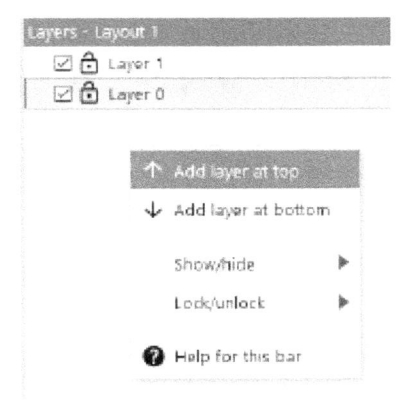

Visually, a viewport can be made as large as or larger than a layout. A layout, however, can never go "outside" of a viewport during display.

A layout can go real large without any practical limits! Each layout can have its own size settings. Because the layers are "merged" for display at runtime, end users won't be able to tell the existence of multiple layers on a layout.

You can selectively make some layers invisible:

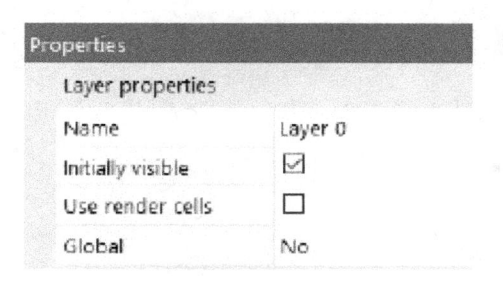

Do note that a layout has an event sheet. A layer does not.

Why is anchor useful?

When you cannot be certain about the runtime screen size it would be difficult for you to set the player object location. This is where an anchor behavior can help.

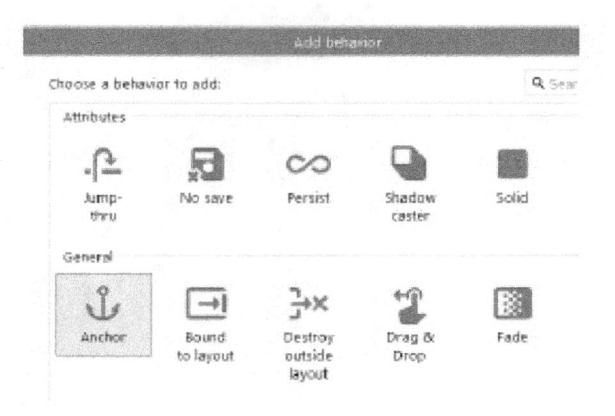

You can set the anchor point to the edges of the viewport so that the relative position of the object can be automatically maintained.

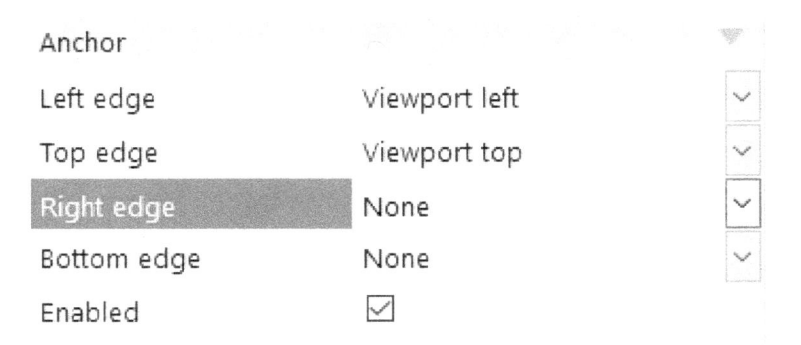

You can enable or disable the anchor at runtime via event action. The official documentation does mention that object with an anchor should be placed on a layer with a parallax setting of 0% x 0% to avoid "lagging behind" when scrolling.

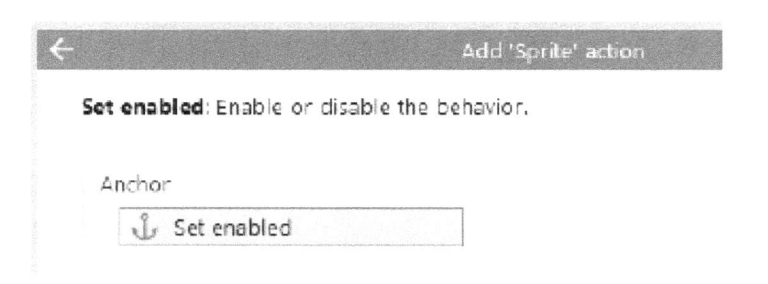

Each object can have one anchor. However, there is no limit on the number of objects that can have an anchor.

Multiple layers and screen effects

Having multiple layers is good if you want to set fancy background scrolling effects. Each layer can have its own scrolling speed, and some layers can even be made stationary.

Settings on layer scrolling are made on a per layer basis, via the Parallax option. 0, 0 means stationary. 100, 100 is ordinary scrolling speed. To be precise, Parallax has 2 values, which are X and Y, and you are free to set them differently, even to a value over 100.

Scroll & zoom		
Scale rate	100%	
Parallax	▶	100% x 100%

Here is another way to achieve the same. When you create a layout, you need to define the width and the height. If, say, this is a platform game with scrolling solely taking place horizontally, you can either scroll the layout or keep the layout static but scroll the background objects.

Special effects can be created by having different groups of background objects (such as clouds) moving at different speed, producing the effect of parallaxing - that is, when parts of the screen scroll faster than the rest.

For example, by adding a bullet behavior to the cloud sprite and set the bullet speed to something slower than the default, you can create a realistic sky scrolling effect. You can place different cloud sprites on different layers, then adjust the opacity and the bullet speed as needed.

An alternative method is to set the cloud sprite to move towards an angle for a distance every *n* milliseconds.

What is the relationship between a layout and an Event Sheet?

The Event Sheet is where you start adding new events to the layout. Put it this way, an event sheet is linked to the current layout. Generally you are given one and only one event sheet per layout.

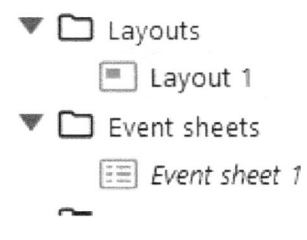

You can right click on an event entry and perform copy & paste of event entries. You can also create INVERTED condition (i.e. a NOT condition) by inverting an existing condition.

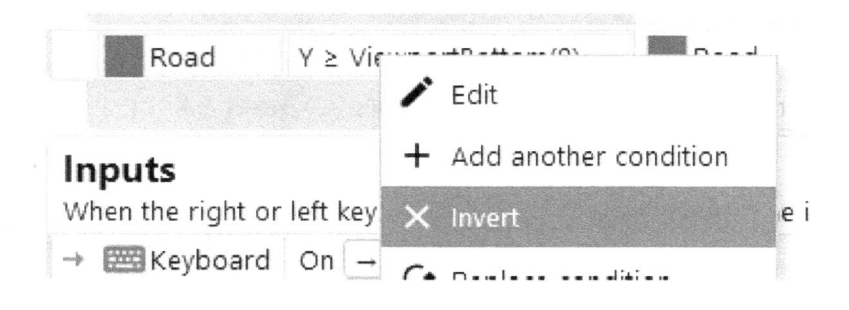

Why should I optimize the event list?

The C3 engine will read through an event list at regular time intervals. The more entries you have in the list, the slower your game is going to run since the program will need to spend longer time in scanning the list.

You should go over the event list from within the Event Sheet. Just read the entries one by one, see if any of them is actually irrelevant or meaningless (no real effects), and make deletion or replacement as necessary. *Programmers in the programming world do this kind of code walk through all the time.*

Watch for conditions that will never happen and delete them as they are useless. Watch for conditions that are in fact mutually exclusive. When two conditions belong to the same event entry and they are contradicting with one another, the event will never take place:

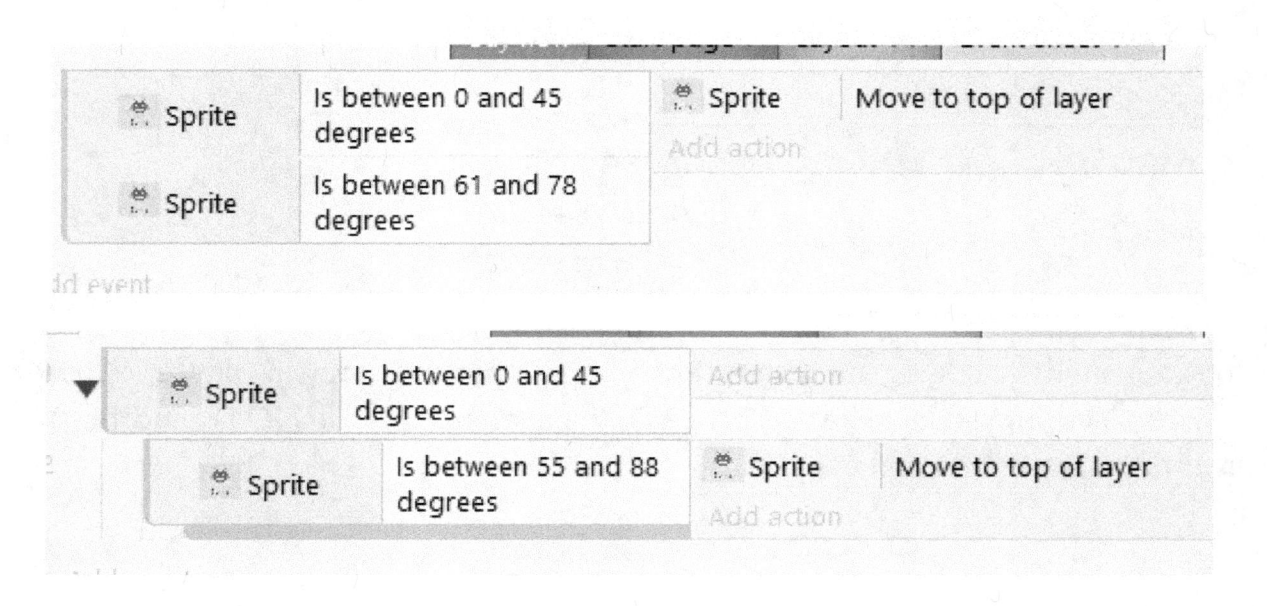

Also watch for conditions that will always happen and determine if the resulting actions will produce a loop crazily. For example, if the condition says an object is on screen and a new object instance will be created as a result - if at runtime this object is almost always on screen then your game will soon be full of newly created object instances.

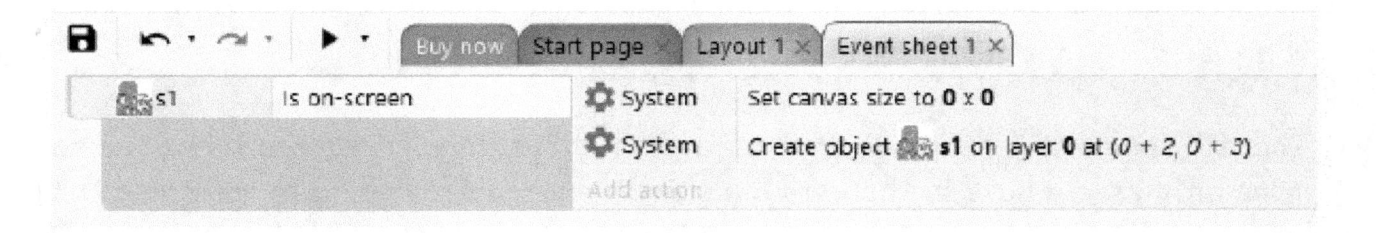

Sometimes a loop will not be producing any visible result but it is in fact wasting processor resources (see the first line of action in the above example – what is the point of setting the canvas size position again and again?).

Implementing IF THEN ELSE in the Event Sheet

IF THEN ELSE logic is possible and easy.

This is an IF THEN logic with an AND among the conditions (both conditions count):

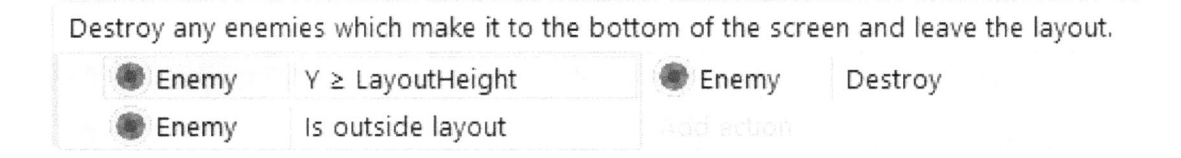

This one has one condition INVERTED (so it becomes an AND NOT):

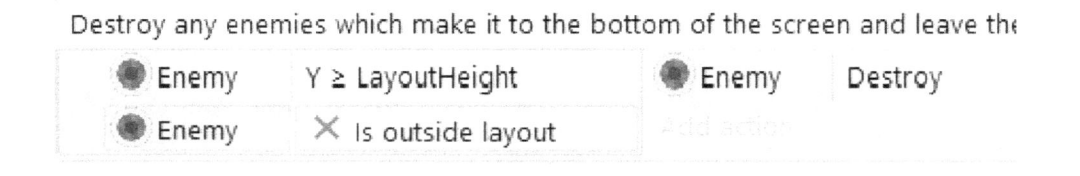

An IF THEN logic with an OR among the conditions (either one condition can trigger the action) can actually be built if you right click and choose Make OR block:

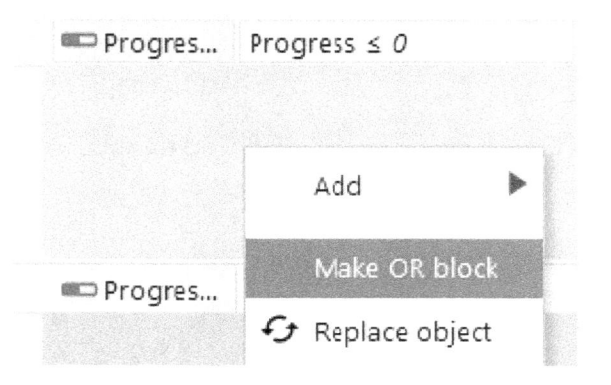

The two sets of conditions shown below are in fact mutually exclusive if you read carefully. Technically this is an IF THEN ELSE.

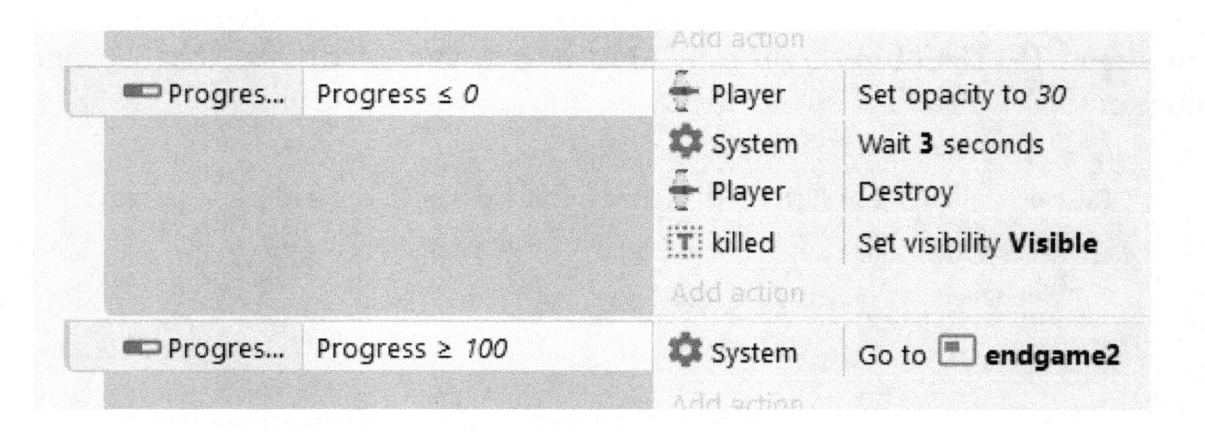

They were not "tied together" though. Style-wise, you may right click and choose Add – Add else to an ELSE between them.

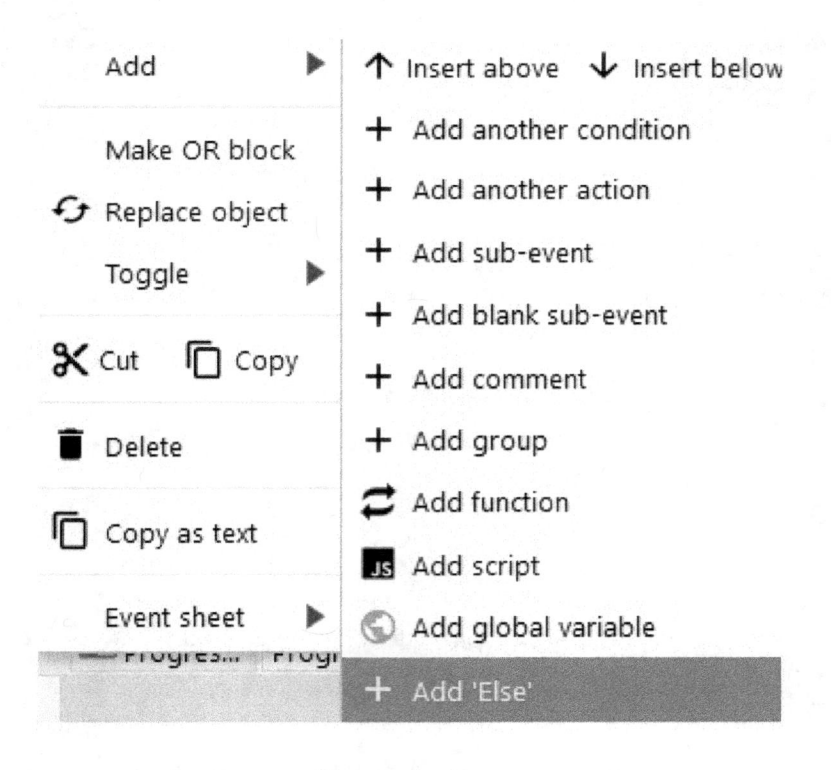

Sometimes you can simulate an ELSE logic by setting up a second condition which has the same content and then have it INVERTED. When the evaluation process flows through these entries, an effect of ELSE will naturally take place.

If you right click on an event, you can choose to add sub event. A sub-event will be evaluated only if the first event it belongs to is evaluated to true. Technically this is NOT an IF THEN ELSE but a longer form of AND. A blank sub event is a place holder which allows you to define the details later.

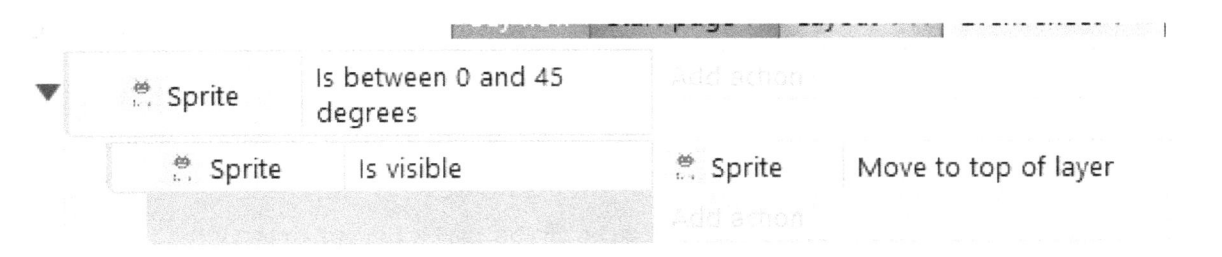

Technically you can have sub sub sub events if you really think that is necessary.

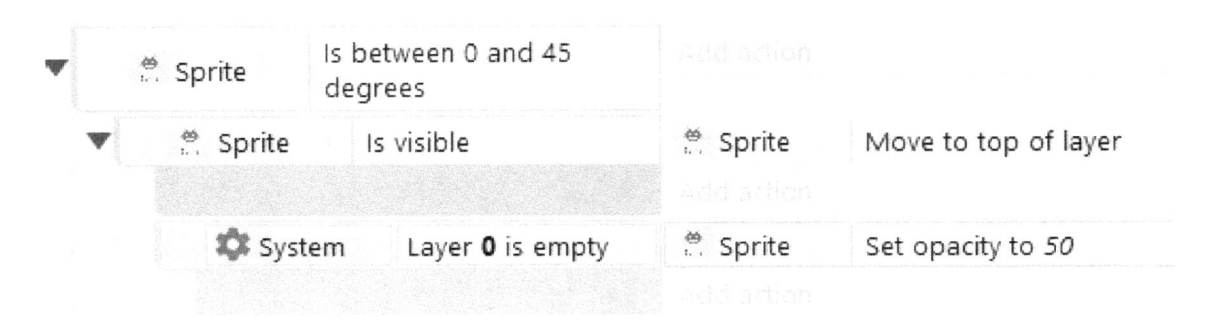

Having blank action is possible. Refer to the example below, there is no action for the first condition – if you do this intentionally to make a visible sprite doing nothing.

Sprite	Is visible	Add action	
System	Else	Sprite	Set opacity to 50
Sprite	Is flipped	Add action	

When multiple conditions are specified on the same line, they form an AND relationships - all conditions need to be matched. There is no need to explicitly set any AND block.

Cloning VS Copying: What is the difference?

In C3, when you right click an object you can choose to clone object type. The new object is one totally independent of the original. If, however, you choose to copy and paste, the new one produced is a duplicate.

Cloning an object means creating a new separated object out of an existing object. Copying/duplicating an object means creating new occurrence(s) of it. Both functions can be accessed when you right click on a sprite.

Copy and Paste = copying/making a duplicate (i.e. a pasted object).
Copy and Paste Clone = cloning.

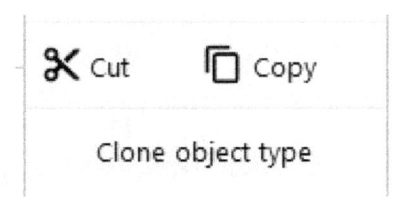

If you modify the look and properties of a pasted object, you are in fact modifying the original source object.

In fact, when you move the source object at runtime the pasted object will also move following the instructions given to the source object. They will always act together. On the other hand, when you produce a pasted clone, the pasted clone becomes its very own object. It has no relationship with the source object at all. One easy way to tell whether an object is a duplicate or a clone -> just check the application properties and see if the object has its own sprite entry. With its own sprite entry, it means it is a totally independent object. Do NOT judge based on the object UID. Even a duplicate will have its own UID.

Effects on duplicated/pasted objects

When an object has, say, 4 duplicates made on the same layout, there is always only ONE shown in the event sheet. In other words, you cannot manipulate each individual duplicate programmatically by default.

Object Instance Variables VS Global Variables

In C3, global variables survive across layouts. If your game has multiple levels, you use global variables to carry over values such as lives, scores ...etc. You right click at the top of the event sheet to add global variables.

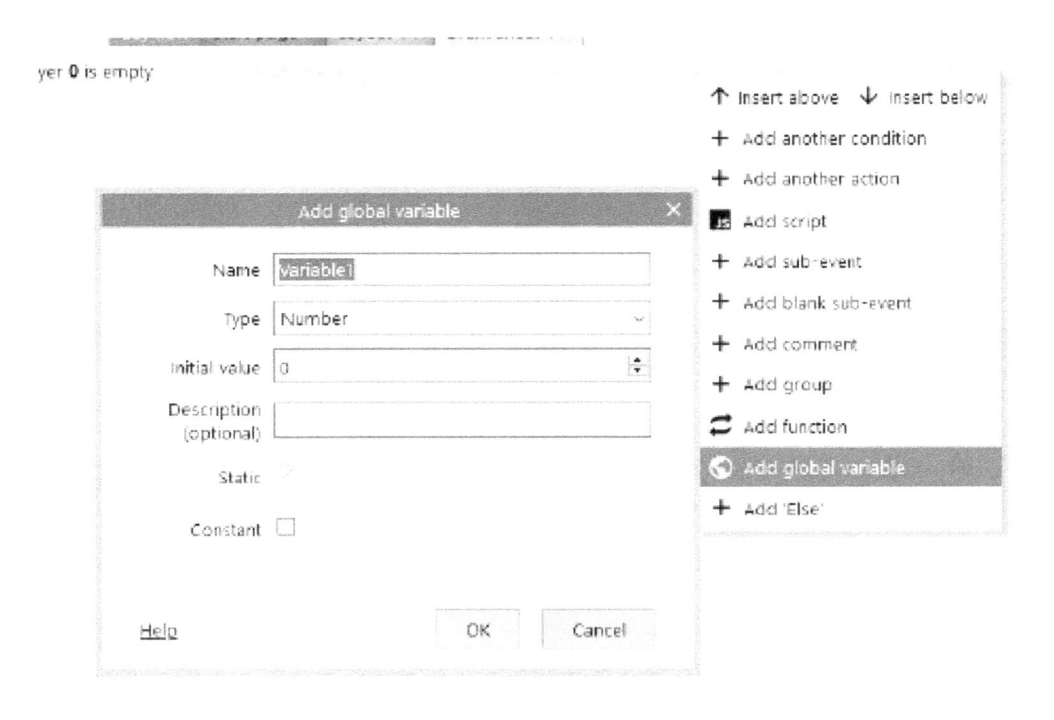

You do not need to make them constant (even though you can, by checking the constant checkbox), unless they are intended to serve as some sort of parameters that are not going to be changed along game execution. On the other hand, an object can have its own instance variable. You can always add instance variables of type number, boolean or text to an object, and can be manipulated via Event conditions and actions.

On the other hand, you may use instance variable to implement variables related to certain objects. For example, the health of an object.

When using global variables you must understand that they are defined through an event sheet, and that an event sheet must be associated with a layout in order to be invoked. Therefore, you must make sure that the layout carrying the event sheet must not skipped when the game runs, or those global variables will not perform as expected.

How about global objects?

When you have multiple layouts and there are screen elements that will be shown on most of these layouts, it makes sense to set an object as global.

By default an object is not global. When an object is not global, you do not need to recreate one for each layout, but you do need to insert it into each layout by hand (you drag it from the list of objects into the layout) manually.

When you have an event sheet that references a local object, the statement will not produce any error as long as the object has been created somewhere in the project. However, if that object is not inserted into the current layout, the event sheet of this current layout will simply ignore the statement that involves the object.

If the object is made global, this object will be present on all subsequent layouts that follow the current layout (that is, if you make an object global at layout 2, this object will also show up in layout 3, 4 and 5 ...etc. But it will not show up in layout 1 unless you manually put it there). You may then manipulate it programmatically.

What can be done with a blank layout?

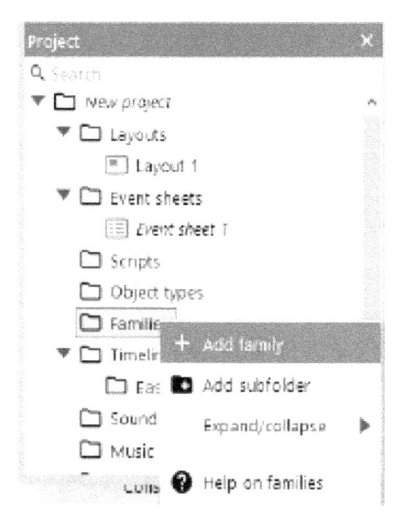

You can use a blank layout right at the start of the game to define all the necessary constants and global variables. Keep in mind, a global variable marked constant is a constant. As said previously, global variables are defined through an event sheet and that an event sheet must be associated with a layout in order to be invoked. This is why you may want to have a blank layout for such purpose.

Object Families VS Container – what is the difference?

In C3 you may use Families to group objects together. You cannot mix and match different object types in the same family though. You may right click on Families and choose Add Family:

With this feature, it would be much easier to define event conditions and actions that affect the entire family. However, the Free edition of C3 does not support this.

When there is a family of objects, you can write actions that affect the entire family, and there is still room for flexibility since you can choose to exclude certain family members on a case by case basis. An object that joins a family can still be individually manipulated whenever you prefer.

If you want to have something that changes the entire family, you must explicitly set your conditions and actions to use the family. A container is different – when an object is part of a container, when it is created or destroyed then every other object in the same container is also automatically created or destroyed. When a condition picks an object in the container, every other object in the same container is automatically picked.

You create a container from an object's properties.

What is "every tick" all about? And what is a timer for?

Just to give you a rough idea, every tick works similar to every 0.1 second...

Instead of using tick as the time unit, C3 allows you to use second, which is more human friendly.

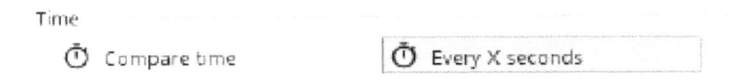

A timer is an object behavior in C3. That means it is tied to an object. It works just like your simple household kitchen timer – it simply counts till it reaches the duration defined in seconds.

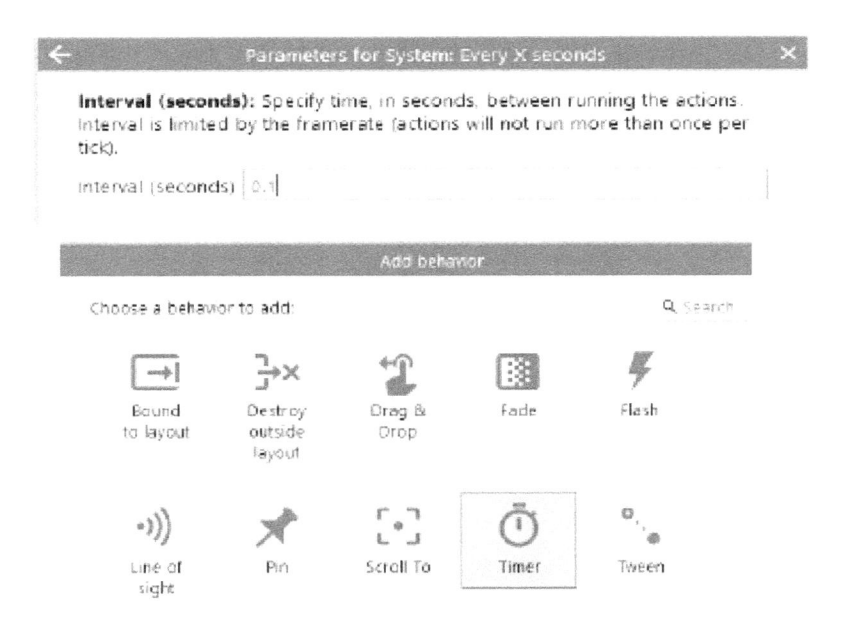

Once added to an object, you use an event action to start it. You can define a tag for identifying the timer.

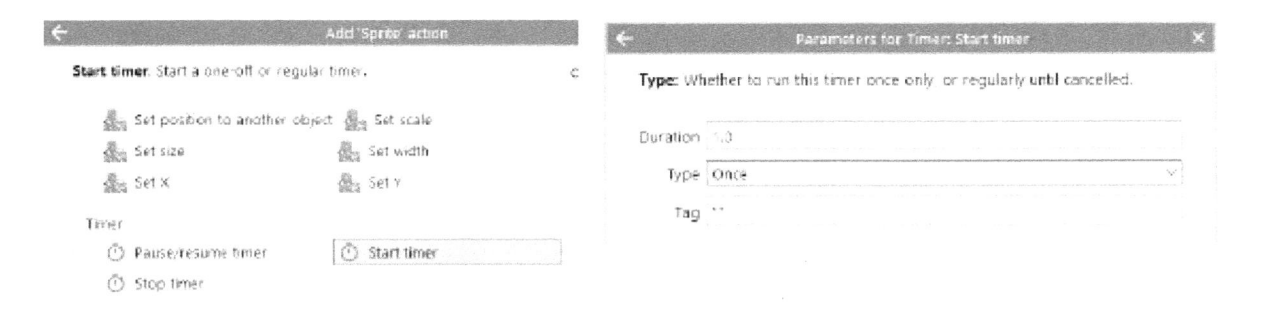

The On Timer condition is trigger when the timer reaches the defined duration.

Timer

⏱ Is timer paused   ⏱ Is timer running

→ On timer

There is no layout by layout timer function in C3. To retrieve the game time, you take the value of time (time is a variable that holds the most current game time) and set it to a variable or a text object. The default is in floating point format, but you can change it to seconds by adding the int function (int means integer ... int (time)). You need to update the variable / text object constantly! And keep in mind, you must do all these via event sheet statements.

Keep in mind, you cannot pause time. Since time is kept updating when the project is started and there is no way to stop it, to find out the layout time you need to have another variable for recording the moment in time the layout is started, then make a subtraction from the latest time to come up with the current layout time.

Yes it is very complicated. Sad.

FYI, you can manipulate the time scale to speed things up or slow things down. We will talk about this later in this book.

Performance Configuration

What configuration should I use for my C3 development station?

A development station for C3 does not have to be real fast and powerful since it is now cloud based. As long as your computer can run web browser in a very stable manner then it will just be fine.

You want to have a very reliable internet connection.

Design time performance VS runtime performance
Design-end performance VS user-end performance

Always keep in mind that design time performance boost is not the same as runtime performance improvement.

Design time performance boost improves productivity (your tools run faster), while runtime performance boost allows the game you create to run faster on the client end. Generally speaking, better hardware can lead to improvement on both.

If your game is going to have a large number of super fancy graphics and animations plus tons of rich objects all showing up at the same time, slower computers may have a harder time working things out. The key issue is this – when you have a very fast development station, all games can run fast in front of you. This can actually mislead you into believing that your game could run as smooth on the user computers.

It may not be wise to assume that all end users are rich enough to own the latest hardware. Also, different target platforms have different performance characteristics.

What other development tools should I install on my computer?

The C3 graphic editor is a pretty basic one. To create very fancy graphics you'll need something more powerful. First you create and save your graphics with a third party tool, then you get them imported into C3 for further editing and customization.

As of the time of this writing, to the best of my knowledge there is no specific virus attack targeting the C3 application files. And if you just keep the files in the cloud, most cloud services have virus scanning features built-in already.

Is GPU performance relevant?

At runtime, GPU can greatly improve performance on the client end but you must realize that not all client platforms have strong GPU. In technical terms, the data rate of writing pixel data to memory is the fill rate. If this fill rate exceeds the GPU memory bandwidth things will slow down. A high fill rate means the GPU is very busy.

Under Project's Properties – Advanced you can set the GPU preference. It is best for you to try out different settings and determine which one works best for your client machines.

Compositing mode	Standard (synchronized
GPU preference	High performance
Downscaling quality	Low power
Max spritesheet size	Default
Editor	High performance

Objects with large areas of transparency and objects with large overlapped areas are wasting GPU resources because even though nothing is actually displayed the processing is still taking place (in other words the GPU has to be busy for producing something with nothing to show).

What is the optimal display resolution for the game to operate at runtime?

The higher the resolution the more workload your display card would have to handle. The good thing about a high resolution setting is that you can squeeze in more objects and let them interact with each others on the same screen. If your game involves movement of all these objects together, things will slow down significantly for sure.

Performance-wise, full screen mode is usually the best. Therefore, if high frame rate is to be maintained, you should only use full screen mode. You are recommended to try out different settings here.

Fullscreen mode	Letterbox scale ⌄
Fullscreen quality	Off
Orientations	Scale inner
Sampling	Scale outer
Pixel rounding	Letterbox scale
Advanced	Letterbox integer scale

Can I select different display modes for different game levels? How should I define the "minimum system requirement"?

You can adjust the layout size on an individual basis. The default layout size is 1708 x 960 but you can always change it to something else.

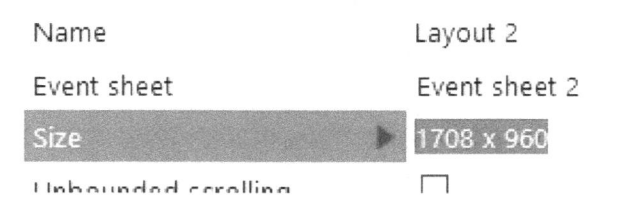

Name	Layout 2
Event sheet	Event sheet 2
Size	1708 x 960
Unbounded scrolling	☐

Just keep in mind, the layout size does not dictate the display size but the viewport size does. Usually the layout size is much larger than the viewport size - scrolling allows you to walk through the entire layout. The viewport size is under Project Preferences though:

BTW, layer scaling can be done programmatically:

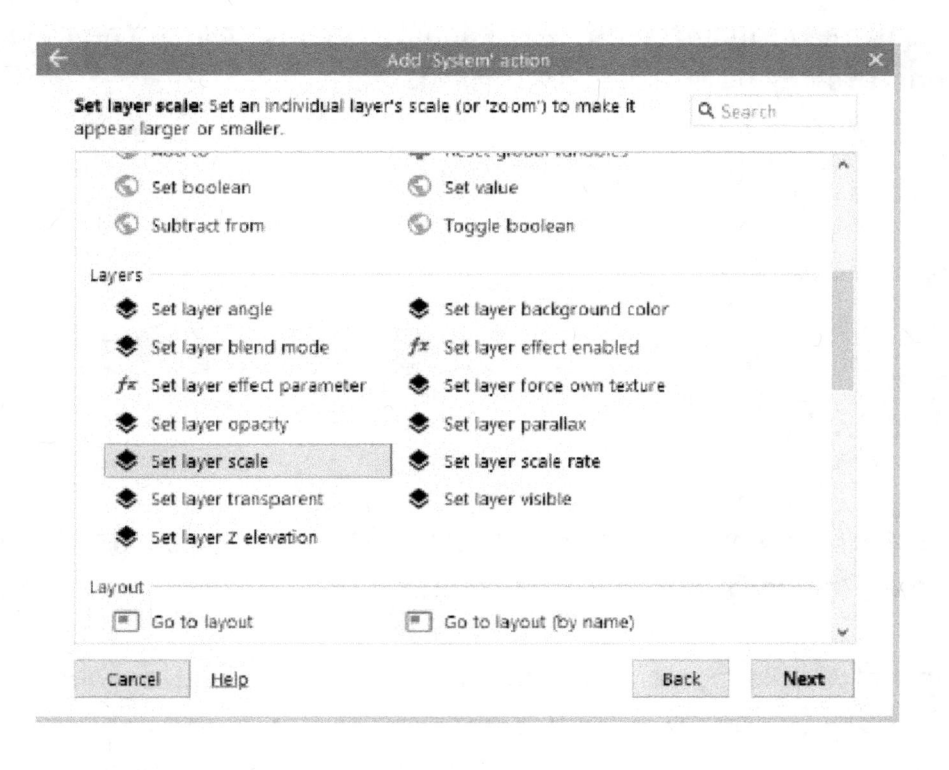

What is blend mode? What about opacity?

Blend mode has to do with manipulating the color values of the foregroup and background objects. Usually you do this when two objects overlap. There are many different blend modes available for you to try out.

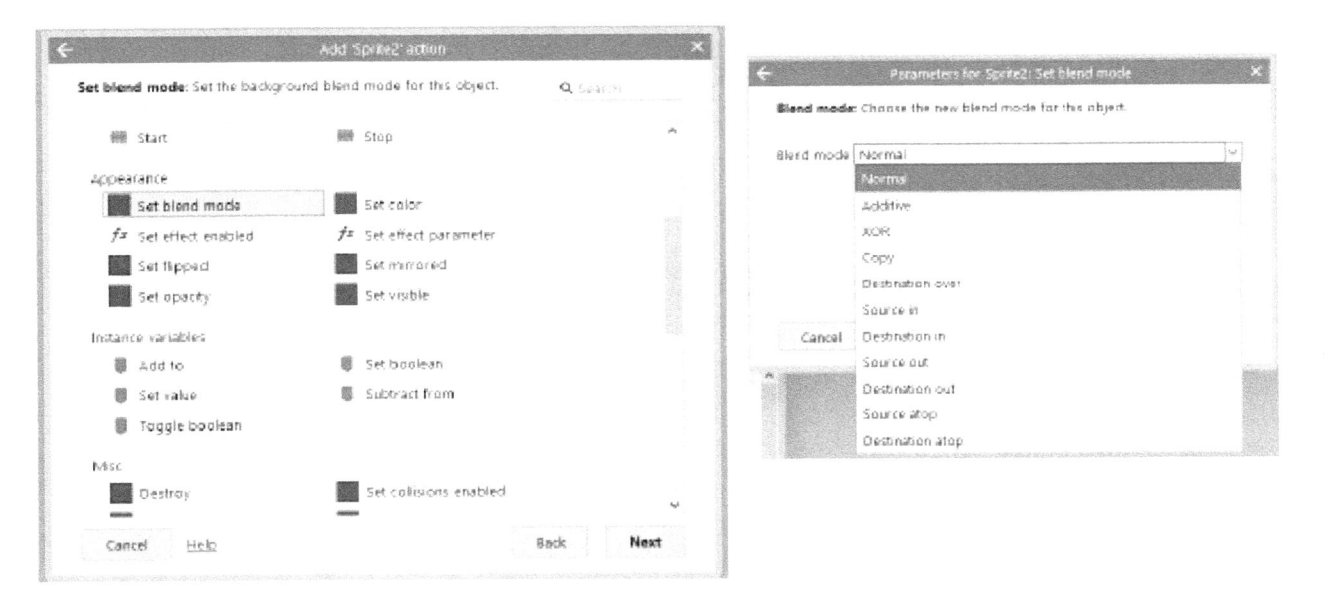

Opacity allows you to adjust the degree of transparency of an object, from 0 to 100.

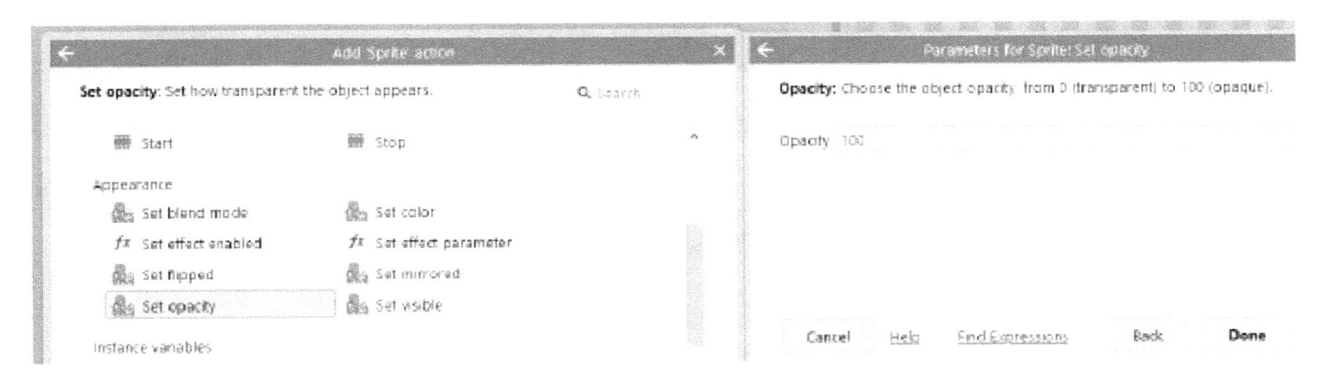

When an object is entirely transparent, it is invisible. You may want to use Set visible instead.

What if I want my object to gradually disappear visually?

The easiest way is to use the Fade behavior.

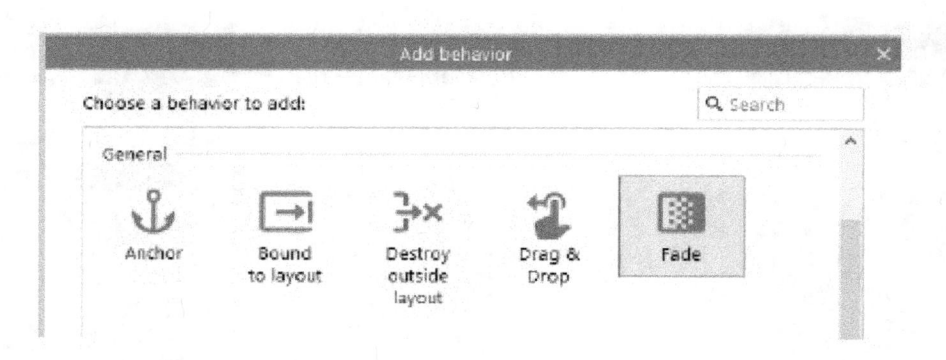

You can set fade in and fade out as well as the time to wait.

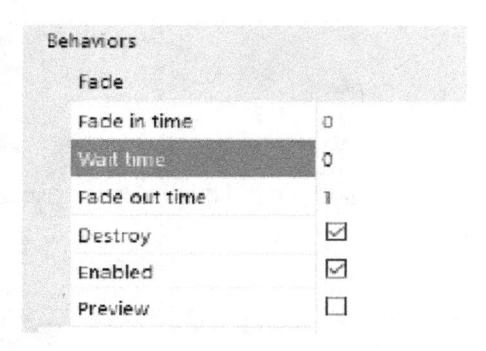

In fact, once this behavior is enabled you can actually use an event action to start it anytime you like:

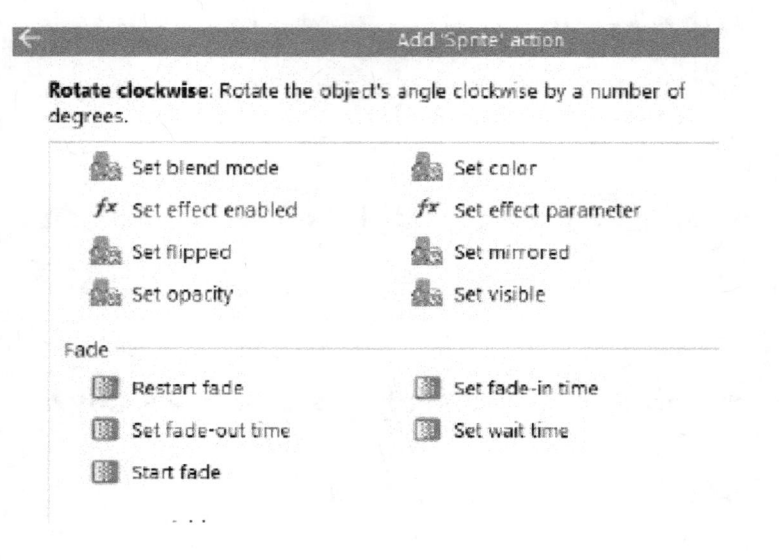

Why would I want to use LoS (Line of sight)?

If you want enemies to be smart enough not to "see" you when there is in fact a wall in between, enable the LoS behavior.

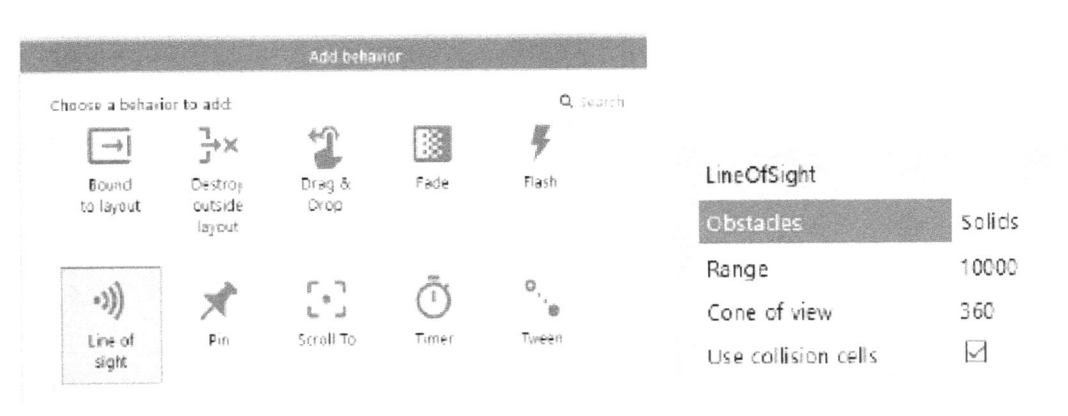

You can choose to treat all solid stuff as obstacles that block your LoS. If you choose custom, only those objects that you specify are used as obstacles. This can be done through event action:

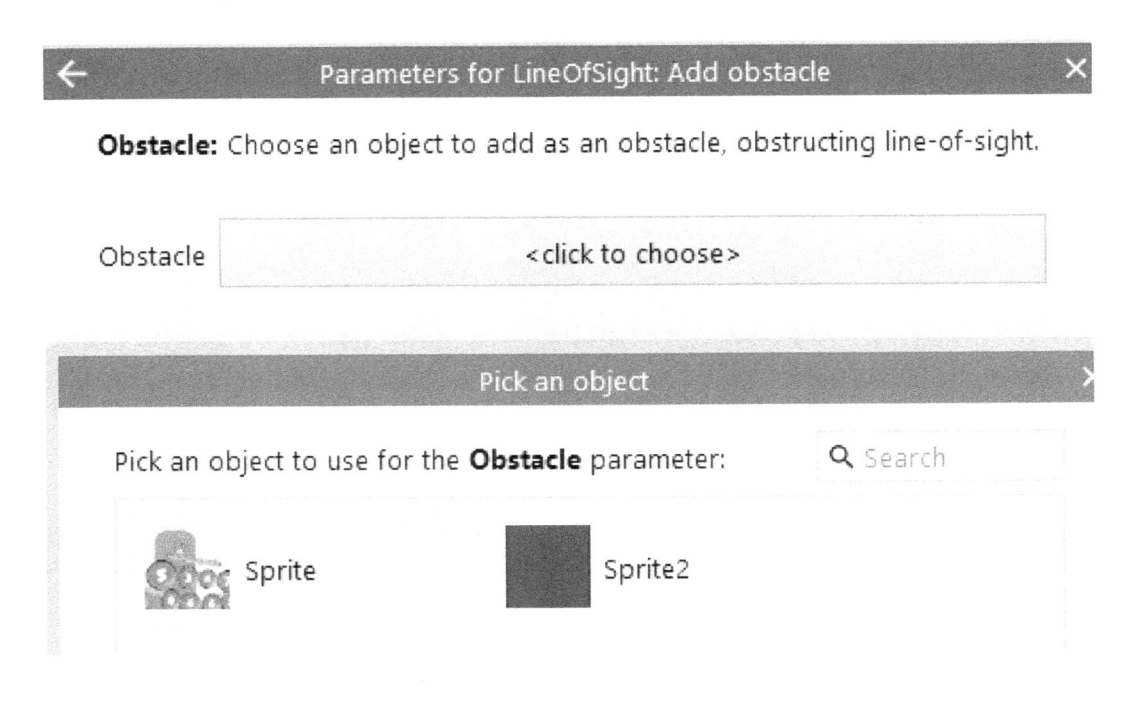

Then you can make use of the relevant event condition to check your LoS with another object:

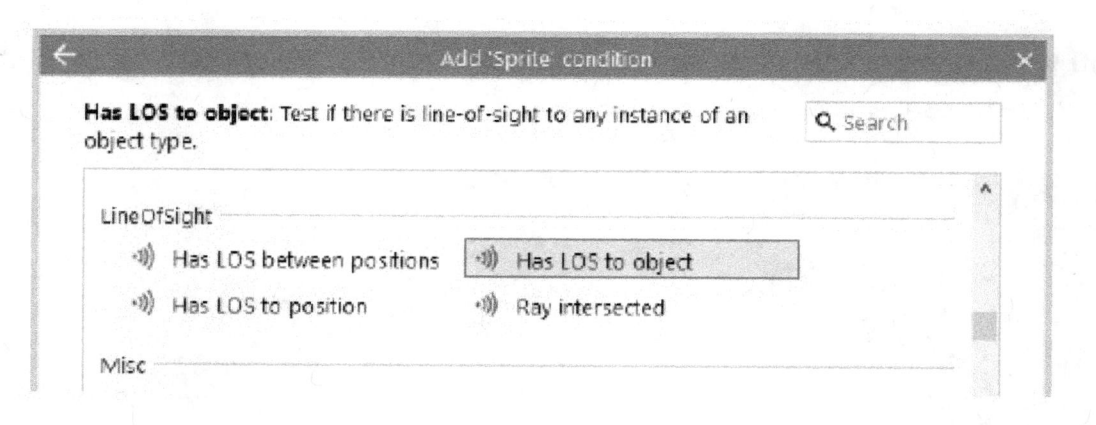

What is the use of adjusting Z elevation?

By adjusting this value you can move your sprite up and down from a top down 3D perspective. To be precise, it can be used to change the visual distance an object is from a camera without affecting the collision area.

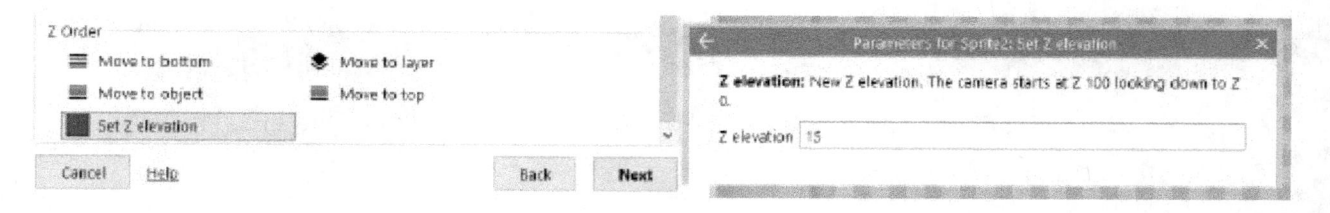

You want to have a basic understanding of Z order in C3 when there are multiple objects and layers involved. Generally, the Z Order increases upwards in a list of objects - objects at the bottom are displayed at the back, while those at the top are displayed at the front.

The Z order bar is not displayed by default but you can enable it via Menu – View – Bars. Not available in the Free edition though.

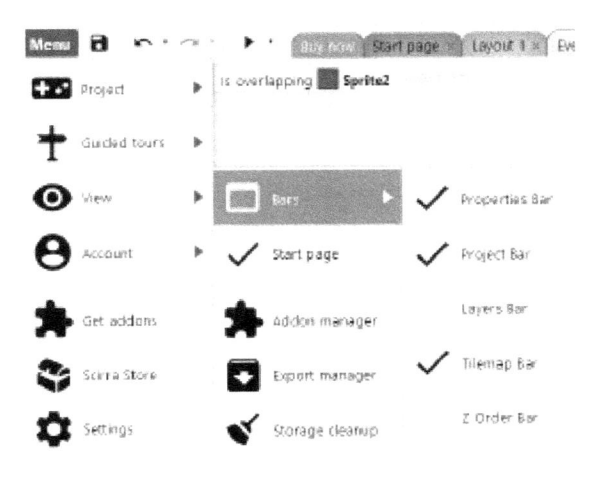

Can I improve screen performance by moving most active objects off screen? What about making them invisible?

Having less active on-screen objects can for sure speed up screen redraw (since there is less to render). HOWEVER, even though off-screen objects (those waiting outside of the current window) are not rendered until they are actually in view, their existence can still cause performance degradation as the same amount of memory is required just for keeping them alive. You do have an option to direct C3 to kill an object that moves too far away – this can be done via Sprite Behaviors:

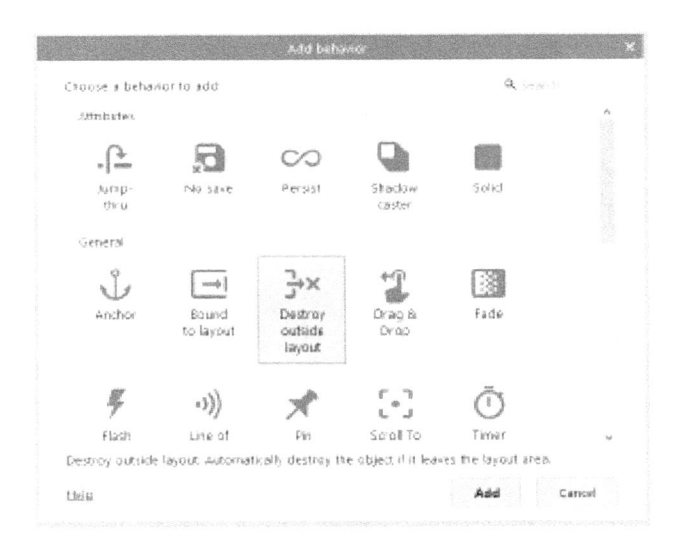

An object that is not visible is still in existence and that all the actions associated with it is still in tact. An invisible object will still collide.

If you do not want to destroy this object but at the same time you do not want it to get in your way, just move it away to somewhere off screen and keep it there.

What are shaders and how do they work?

Shaders are special programs capable of describing the traits of either a vertex or a pixel. A vertex shader deals with the position, texture coordinates, and colors of a vertex. A pixel shader, on the other hand, deals with the color, z depth and alpha value of a pixel. These programs can be used to modify graphical images at runtime such that special effects can be implemented.

TO produce the effect of shader you can use the Shadow Caster behavior which is tied to your desired sprite to cast a shadow from a Shadow light object.

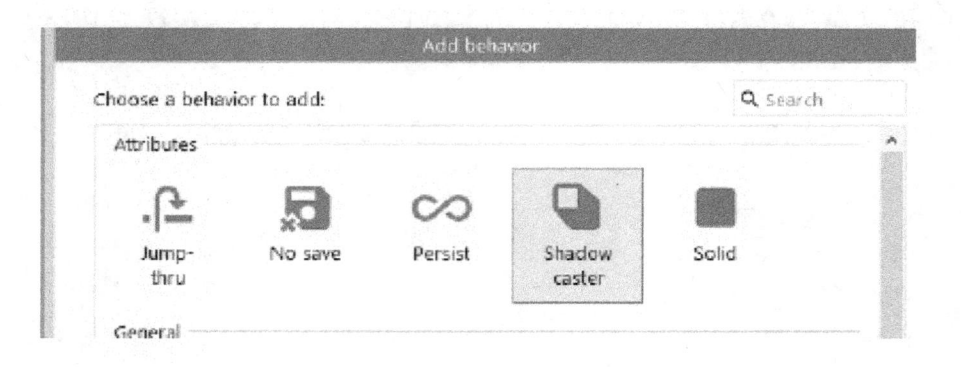

You can create a shadow light object via Insert Object. This is a special object that renders shadows adjacent to objects with the Shadow caster behavior. By default a shadow light will cast shadows off all shadow casters unless you specifically use tag.

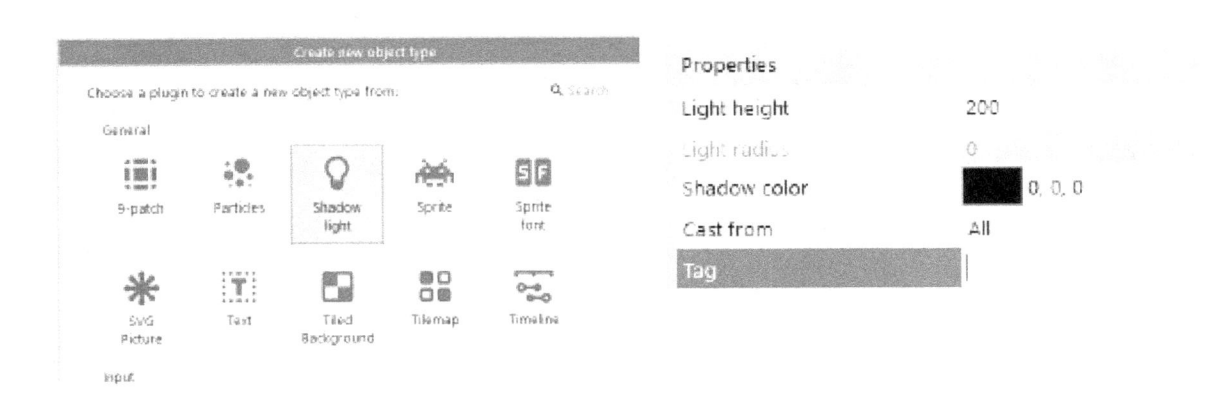

You can have multiple shadow light objects per layout but beware of the performance drag.

What is anti-aliasing all about?

Anti-aliasing refers to the technique of minimizing the distortion artifacts (the edgy look) when representing a high resolution image at a lower resolution or vice versa (which is quite common when an image is being resized). It works by blending the boundary pixels of the image in question. You can see a difference in display quality of textual data when this option is being manipulated at runtime (it does add significant workload to your display hardware). Normally it is something primarily for 3D in realtime.

When you crop a sprite image using the builtin editor, a small transparent border is automatically produced around the edge of the image to achieve similar result without affecting processor workload.

What are the major runtime performance obstacles?

Assuming the computer and the OS are properly configured, major runtime performance obstacles of a C3 game would include:

- stupidly complicated logics or endless loops, which keep the CPU busy doing computation all the time
- unrealistic screen details, which tax the display function heavily
- a very slow web browser

Most 2D action games shouldn't require intensive computation unless there is some serious flaw in the program logic. Unrealistic screen details and the extensive use of animation objects may slow things down and this is more or less a design issue.

Game Design

Why would a *single large object be counter-productive at runtime?*

In theory, a one-piece type large object is bad performance-wise. The primary problem is on screen redraw – a small tiny change somewhere on it would require that the whole object be redrawn. Redrawing a large object all the time is no fun at all.

Advances in computer hardware performance had made the rendering of very large objects a relatively less stressful process.

If you can break this single large object into multiple smaller objects, unnecessary screen redraw can be kept to an absolute minimum. *However, you need to define logics to link (or bind) these smaller objects together.*

C3 has a feature known as Container, which allows you to use smaller objects to form a bigger object (they call it composite object).

What is the difference between an origin and an image point? How to use them?

In C3 we have origin and image points. Each object can have one origin but multiple image points. An image's origin is its point of rotation. There is only one per sprite. Image points are the focal points in the image. In the picture editor, you can specify multiple image points for a sprite. As a point in the sprite image you can refer to, you may choose to specify that new objects be spawned from the image point (image you want to spawn new bullets from a specific location of a gunship). When editing an event you can also specify X Y location basing on the image point location.

You right click to add image points as needed.

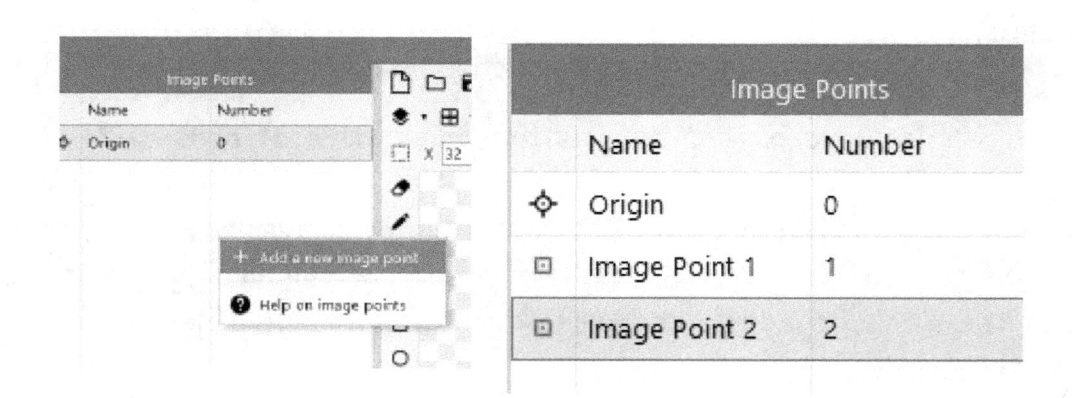

When you spawn a new object you can specify which image point the new object will be created from:

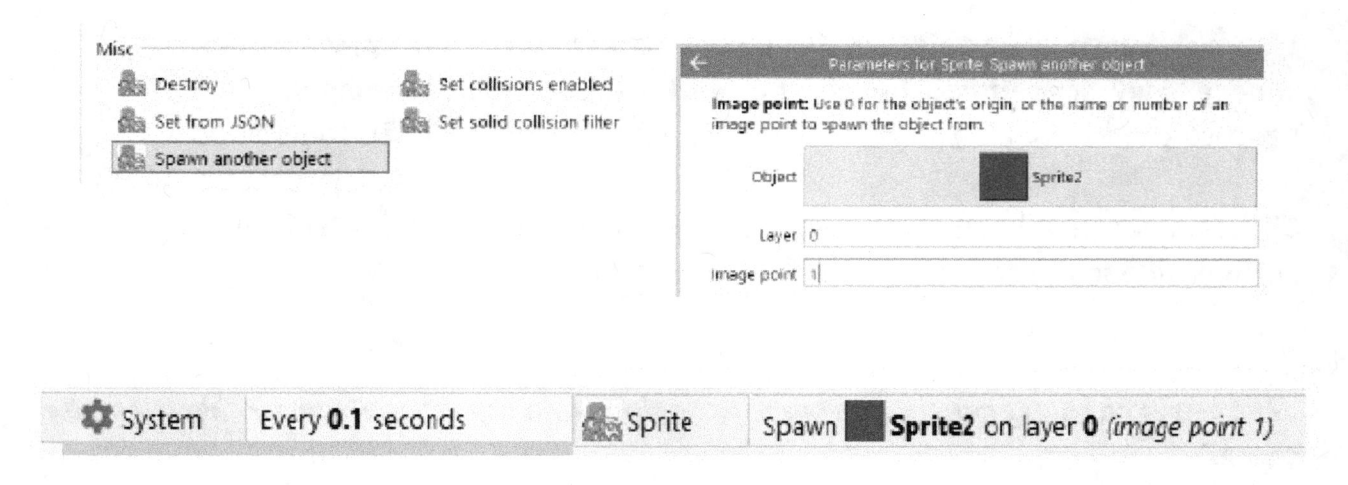

| System | Every **0.1** seconds | Sprite | Spawn | **Sprite2** on layer **0** *(image point 1)* |

What is spawning?

Spawning means creating a new object out of it. You define the object involved, the layer it resides on, and the relevant image point to use. Say you want your player object to shoot a bullet. Assuming the player sprite has the proper image point defined, from the event work sheet you choose the spawn another object action and specify the use of a bullet object for spawning.

How to assign movement to a character sprite?

In C3, with a sprite selected you can add a behavior. You cannot have multiple movement types nested for an object. Note that 8Direction is for use with the player character only.

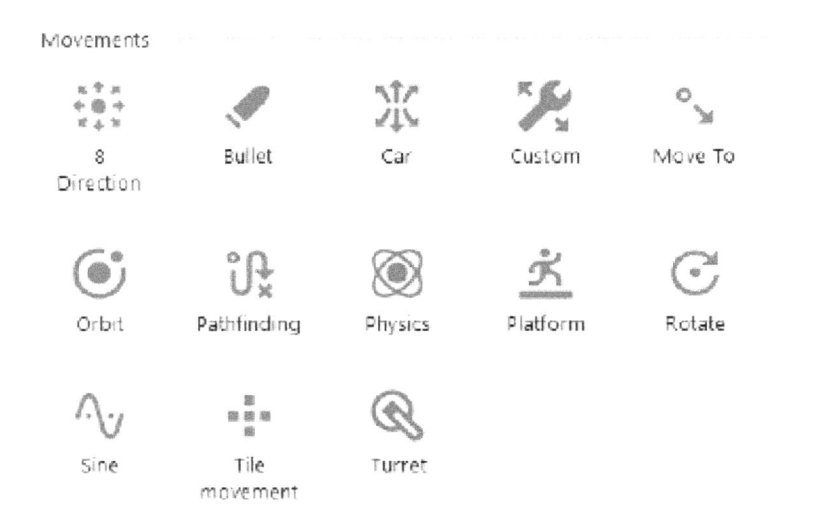

Can I have multiple 8Direction movements assigned to different characters at the same time? Any alternative?

Yes you can. However, they will all respond to your movement commands together at the same time. To allow a different character to act according to different inputs, you may need to use a keyboard related condition. For example, when a key is pressed, the character sprite player 2 will move at a particular angle for a particular distance. To achieve this, you must first insert the keyboard object into the layout before you can build an "on key pressed" action:

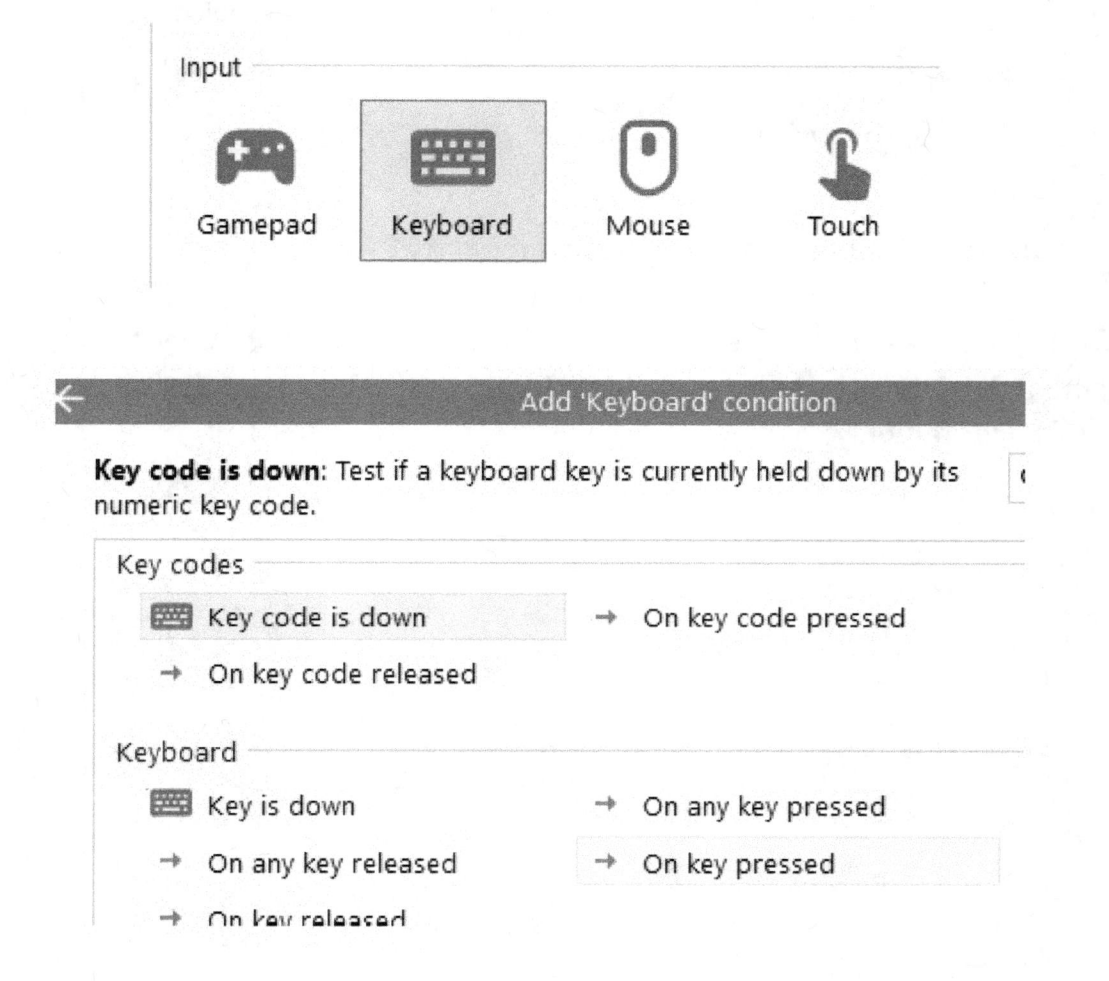

How to assign movement to a bullet character sprite? How about hitting a target?

First of all a "master" bullet should be placed outside of the layout. It is not supposed to be seen. Then you select the bullet behavior for it, and then define an event to allow spawning of it from another sprite (such as from the player character or from a gun).

When the bullet hits the target, a collision event occurs. An explosion object is spawned from the bullet accordingly.

Unless you have configured otherwise, you do not need to explicitly enable collision. After that, the bullet (only this particular bullet, NOT the master

bullet) is destroyed via the Destroy action. It will only destroy the instance that calls it.

How to ensure that the "master" bullet and other "master objects" that were placed outside will not be visible?

The best way is to ensure your player will not be able to walk outside of the layout. This has to do with restriction on screen scrolling. When the unbounded scrolling option is enabled, the player will be able to scroll to the edges, making things outside of the layout visible. My recommendation is that you should always leave the unbounded scrolling option unchecked. Note that this is an option under Layout properties.

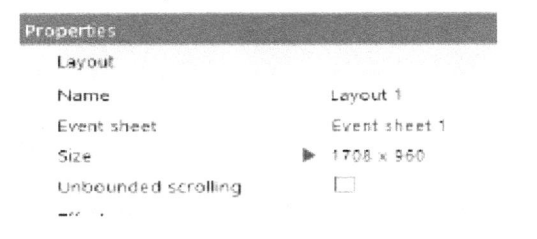

How do I allow for multiple bullets to be propelled towards different directions at the same time?

You are always free to spawn bullets from different image points (if you have defined multiple image points for the player).

Why should I implement multiple layers?

Say your game allows scrolling, and you want some dashboard items (score, health ...etc) to be presented on the screen. You can implement scrolling on one layer, and then present the dashboard stuff on another layer that has no scrolling allowed.

C3 does not classify layers based on functions. You are free to do whatever you want on the new layer you add.

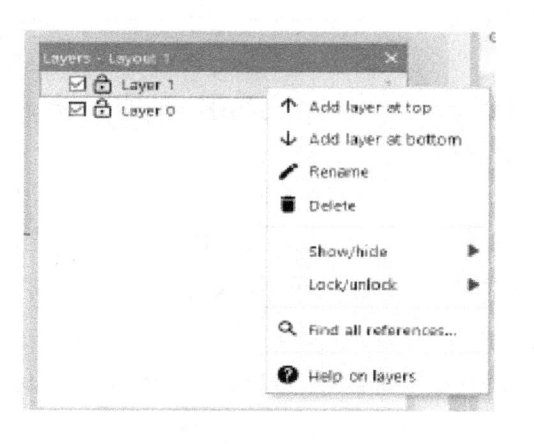

Note that when the Appearance is set to Transparent, it simply means the layer's background is transparent. Everything that resides on the layer is still visible.

Sometimes you may need to arrange the display order of layers in order for certain items to be displayed. You can do so via simple drag and drop.

Collision detection on the same layer...

Collision detection is pretty straight forward. By default, collision detection is on a per pixel basis – you do NOT need to explicitly define any boundaries for your sprites. In fact it is always recommended that you use the default. Say the player is round shaped. If you use any rectangular boundary for collision detection, the outcome will become inaccurate.

Collision detection across different layers...

Collision detection across layer is automatic, nothing special needs to be done to enable it.

What is special about background tiling?

If you are doing backgrounds, the traditional technique is to use tiles. Properly designed tiles have patterns that look extremely well. *You can think of tiles as textures that have been specially formatted to blend together really well.*

The logic behind background tiling is simple. Say you have a background consisting of one huge brick wall. Using one single big bitmap for it would be a waste of memory UNLESS each single brick of the wall is unique. If the bricks are more or less the same, a memory-saving method of building up such wall would be to paint the same brick repetitively on screen for forming the wall.

The general advice out there for background tiles is to make tile units in pixel squares of no larger than 256x256 for efficient processing to take place on the computer without sacrificing visual quality (power-of-2 texture sizes such as 2, 4, 16, 128 ...etc are usually the best).

In C3, configuring tiled background is easy since tiled background is an object you can place onto a layer. So is tilemap. And they all have their editors builtin for you to play with.

General

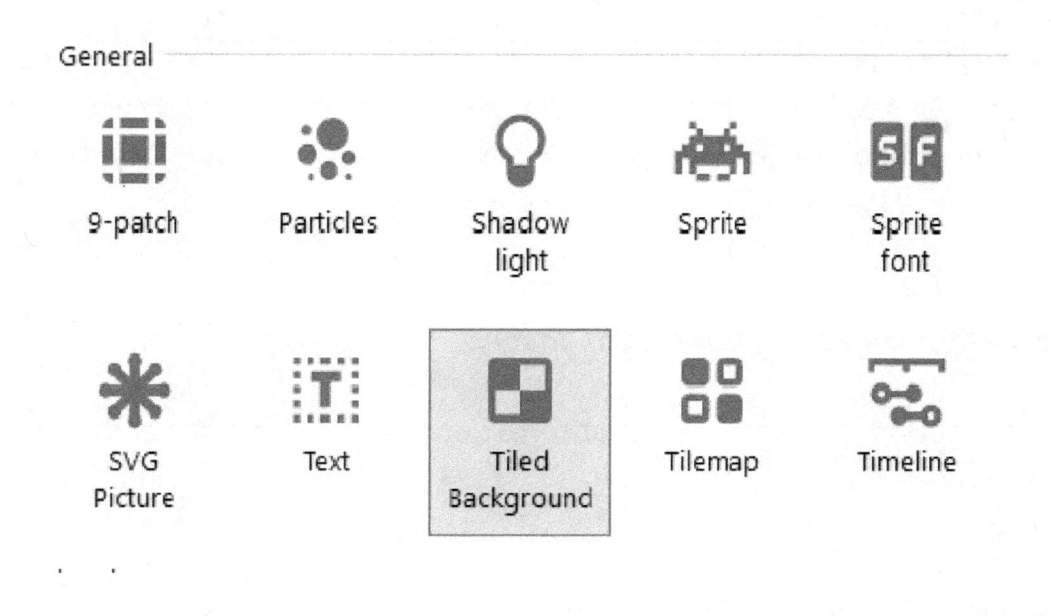

9-patch   Particles   Shadow light   Sprite   Sprite font

SVG Picture   Text   Tiled Background   Tilemap   Timeline

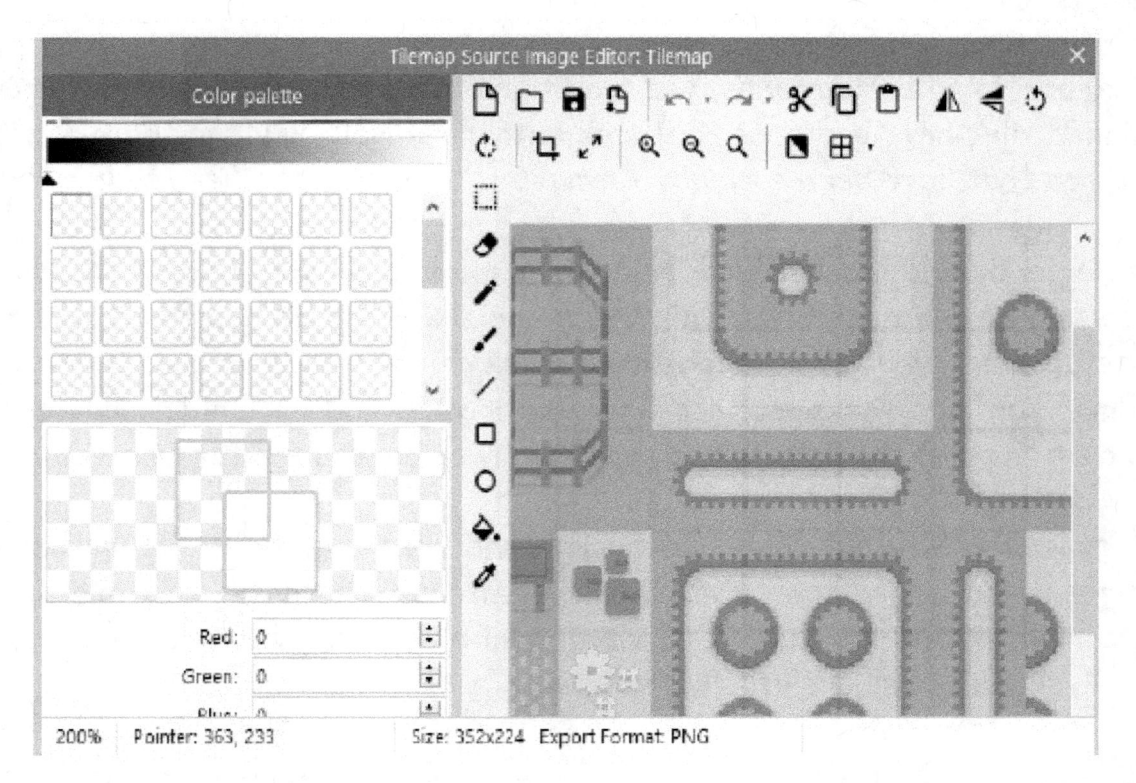

Properties   ✕

Plugin	Tilemap	⌃
Common		▽
Position	▶ 0, 0	
Size	▶ 1708 x 960	
Opacity	100%	
Color	☐ 255, 255, 255	
Layer	Layer 0	⌄
Z elevation	0	
Z index	1 of 2	
UID	3	
Instance variables		▽
Add / edit	Instance variables	
Behaviors		▽
Add / edit	Behaviors	
Effects		▽
Blend mode	Normal	⌄
Add / edit	Effects	
Container		▽
No container	Create	
Properties		▽
Image	Edit	
Initially visible	☑	
Tile width	32	⇕
Tile height	32	⇕
Tile X offset	0	⇕
Tile Y offset	0	⇕
Tile X spacing	0	⇕
Tile Y spacing	0	⇕
More information	Help	

A single large object VS a group of smaller objects linked together: a design time decision?

Say you need to create a big boss, which is a large tank like spaceship with 3 tank turrets capable of shooting in different directions. If you create this big boss as a single active object, all graphics and animations must be created as a whole, and the actions of the 3 turrets must be pre-planned. If the boss is to react to your attack, the 3 turrets will have to react together in a pre-defined manner since they all belong to the same object. Such design is simple and straight forward, and you will unlikely run into bugs. Flexibility and controllability are lacking though.

If instead of making it as a single object you come up with a 4-piece design consisting of the spaceship object, the turretA object, the turretB object and the turretC object. Now you can have individual control over each essential part of the big boss, since each object can have different actions for reacting to different event conditions. Visually, you can "link" them together simply by manipulating their positions and their animation sequences through the event work sheet (say, turretA must always be in a position which is X,Y to the spaceship object).

See this massive scale spaceship with lots of individual turrets on it? Each of these turrets can shoot and be hit on an individual basis. Therefore they should be implemented as individual active objects "bound" to the main spaceship body.

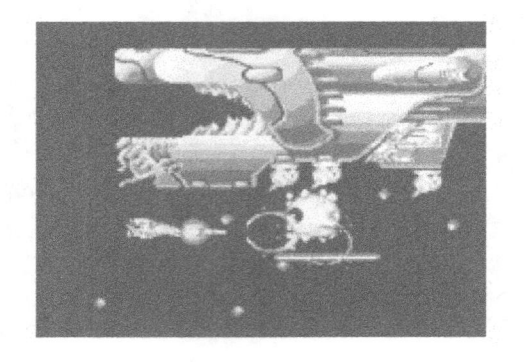

This approach gives flexibility and controllability. HOWEVER, it may just be outright improper for certain types of enemy character. Say if the big boss is a Godzilla, how would you link the head, body, tail, and craws together satisfactorily?

Remember the big boss in R-Type? With a boss of this size and complexity I would definitely implement it with at least three different objects – the head, the body and the tail. In fact, given the complexity and nature of the tail I may even consider to "assemble" the tail from multiple smaller objects!

More on "binding" objects together...

Mario needs to ride on the dinosaur. That means the two objects must first collide and overlap with each other. The event will need to cover this condition, plus any other special condition (such as pressing a particular key).

Once the intention to ride is confirmed through meeting these conditions, the two objects can play their corresponding special animation sequences (to make it look like Mario is actually riding on the dinosaur). The dinosaur can also be bound to Mario (through relative positioning) so that Mario is in control of all the movement. What that means is that Mario is still doing all the actual running and jumping (probably with increased speed and strength), but just that it looks like it is the dinosaur that handles all the tough works.

An event may be put in place such that when the couple receives a hit, Mario will get knocked off and the binding broken. In any case the two would remain as separate objects at all time.

If you use the C3 container feature, keep in mind you cannot programmatically add or remove objects to and from the container.

Configuring big bosses for your levels

As previously said, some big bosses are better to be created and animated in a one-piece form. Say you have a Godzilla monster. You want to configure it in such a way that its head is weaker than its belly. In other words, a hit on the head is going to hurt more and let it scream differently.

An easy way to do this is to make use of several transparent dummy objects. Have these objects bound to the corresponding body parts of the Godzilla. They take the hits and react on behalf of the true Godzilla body. Because they are separate objects, you can configure each of them differently and uniquely. Once the predefined total hit threshold is reached, an event can trigger an action to terminate the Godzilla.

The fancy way of carrying a weapon

When your character is small, the action of holding and shooting a gun by the player object is usually done in one-piece with different animation sequences.

When the character is big (and when you want to allow for fancy operations such as exchanging/swapping weapons with other objects, weapon damage when getting hits …etc), it may be a good idea for the weapon to be implemented as a separate object.

The weapon can be bound to the player's location or image point, and actual shooting can be done by the weapon itself (it takes player command directly by "listening" to keyboard events).

Fine tuning collision with solid object...

You make a sprite object solid by adding a solid behavior.

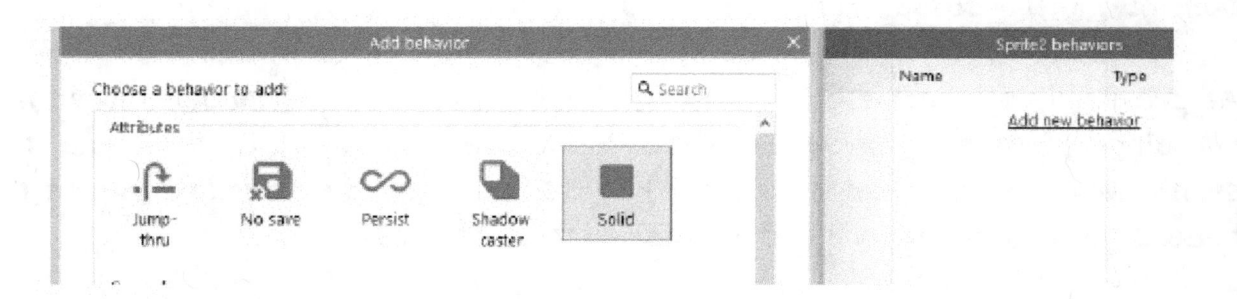

The solid state can be enabled or disabled programmatically.

Tag is very useful because you can use it to identify the object for inclusion or exclusion in collision detection with another object (ie collision filtering – configuration is done on a per object basis).

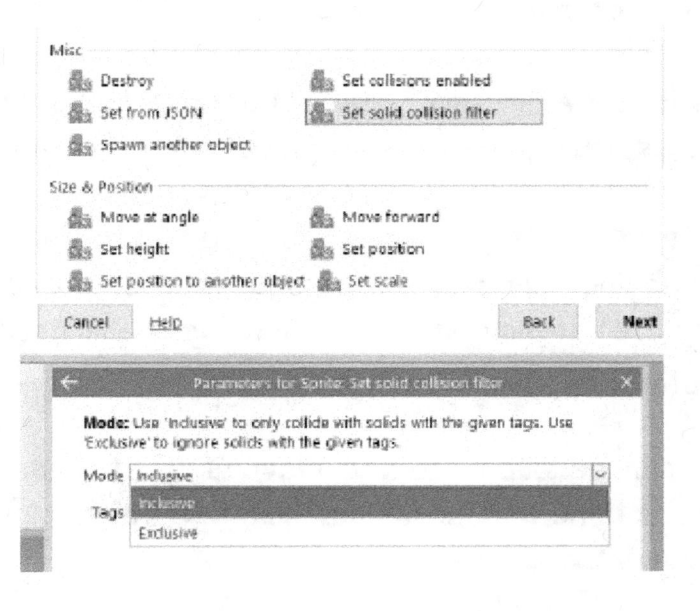

How to setup slow motion or speedup mode?

You can manipulate the timescale. At the project level you can use the system action known as Set Time Scale. 1.0 is normal, 2.0 means 2X, ...etc.

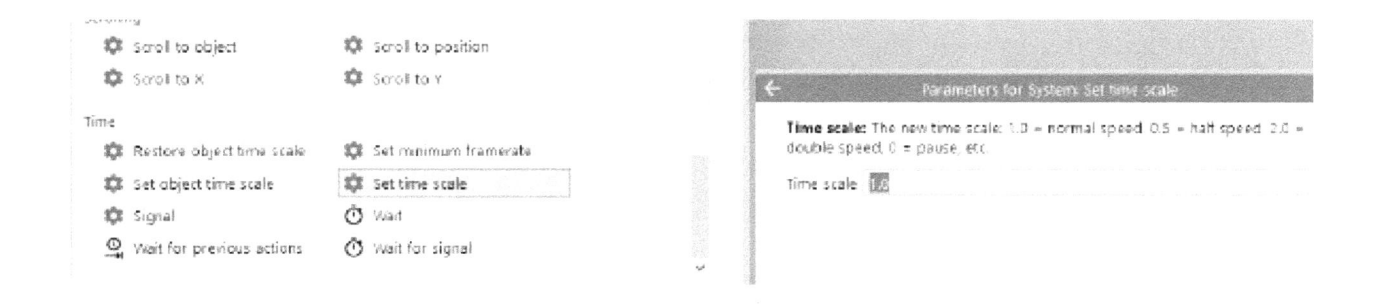

Or you can slow things down or speed things up per object via Set object time scale.

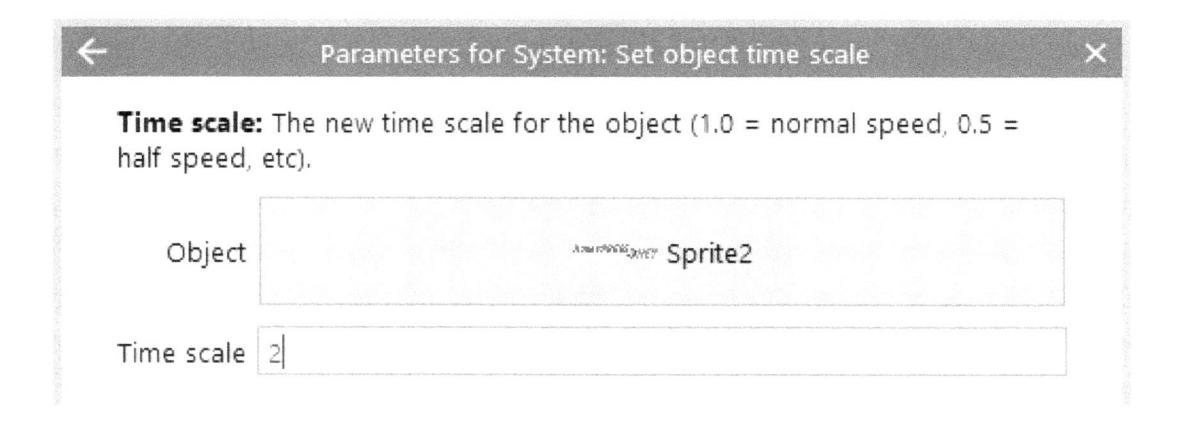

To avoid confusion you should be very careful playing with the time scale.

How to use private variables?

An object can have its own private variables. You use private variables to keep track of things, such as life, health, score ...etc. The variables defined can be used in event conditions / actions accordingly.

Private variables are in fact instance variables. They are tied to a particular object. You add them via the object's properties. They can be boolean, number of string. Practically, they are most useful as numbers, for counting/discounting values.

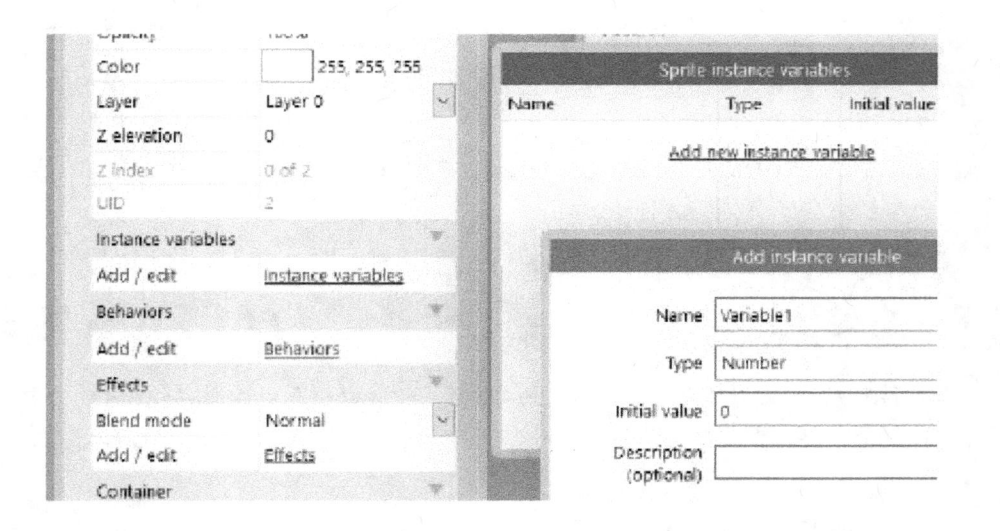

Because they are private, their name has to be unique only within the context of the object they belong to. The object's event actions can only manipulate its own instance variables.

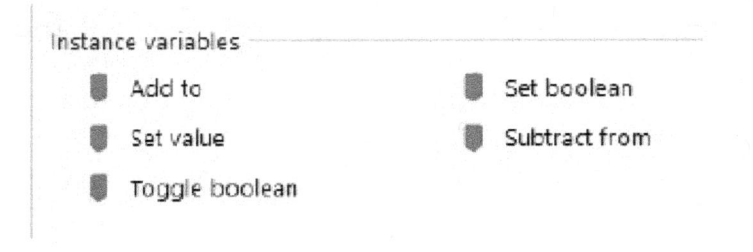

How to play animation and/or movie in the game?

You can use the Video object.

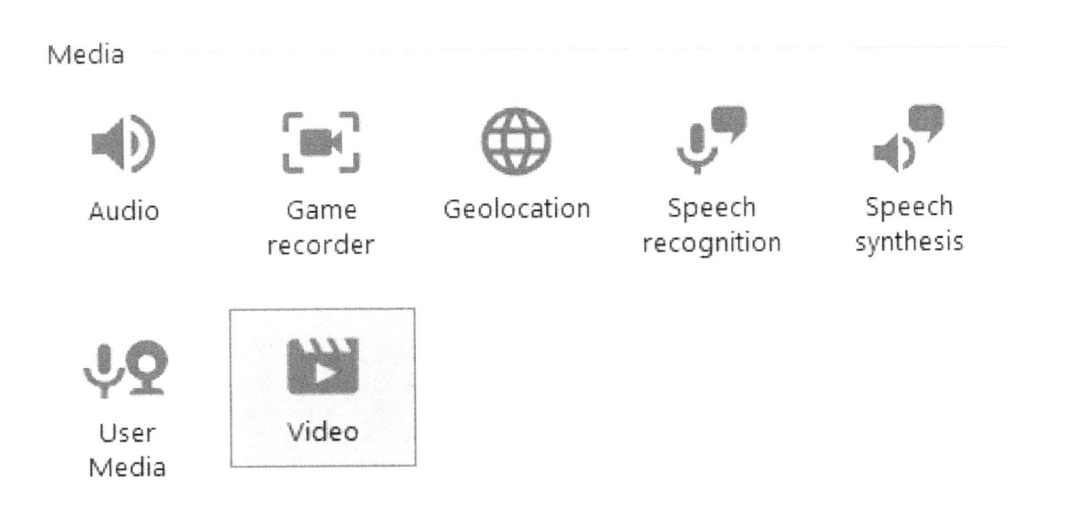

You can specify the size and location of the playback. To activate the playing and loading of file, you may use event action. Properties of the object can be specified at design time or at runtime but you need to know the file format supported, which are WebM (royalty free media format for HTML5), Ogg (open source container format for audio and video) and H264 (widely used codec for media).

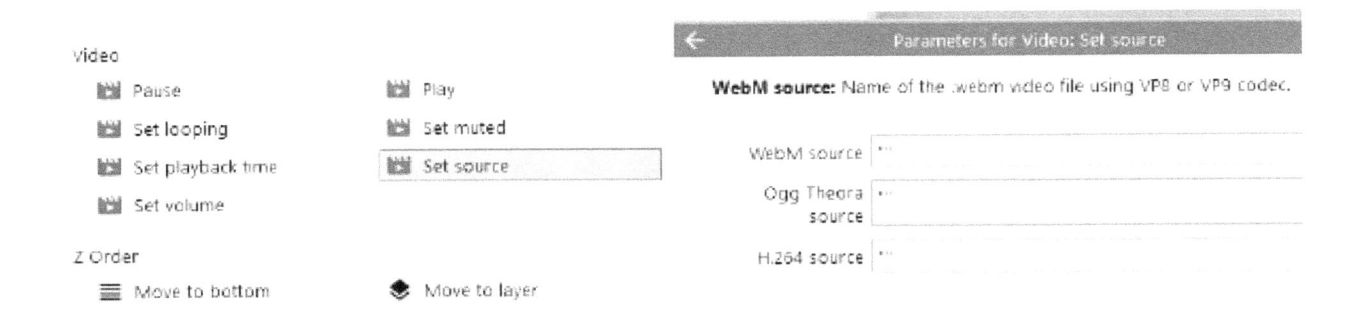

How to play sound and music in your game?

You can use the Audio object. It does support timescale - game timescale can speed up or slow down playback!

Name	Audio
Plugin	Audio
Properties	▼
Timescale audio	Off ☑
Save/load	Off
Play in background	On (sounds only)
Latency hint	On (sounds and music)

There are many event actions you can use with this object. It is a good idea to preload musics early in the game to ensure smooth playback.

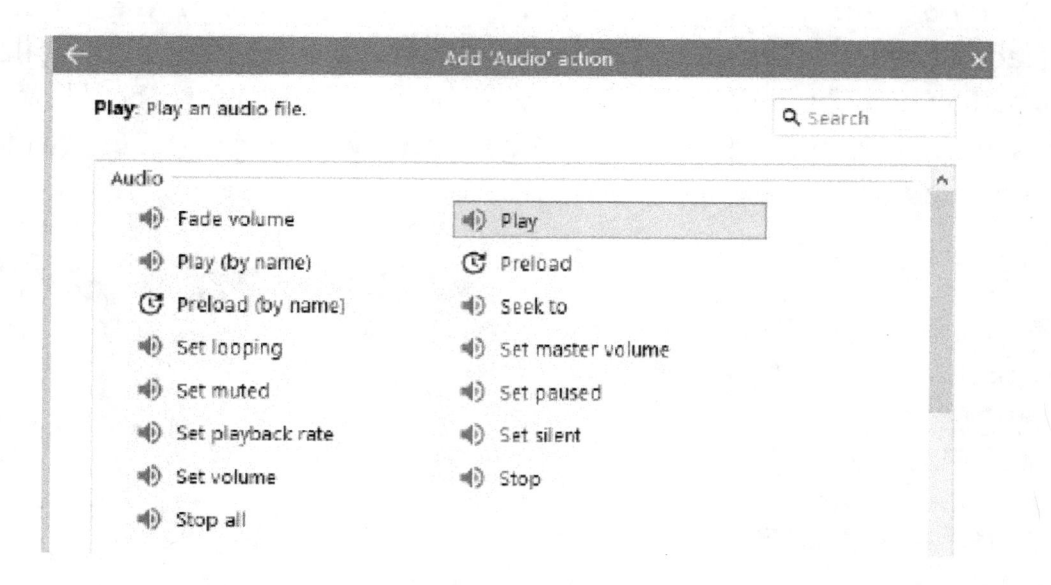

You do not use WAV files for everything as they are relatively large in size. MP3 files (in MP3 format) or WMA files (in WMA format) can be used as background music since they are way smaller. In any case these are the supported formats. You must import them into C3 first (right click Music then choose Import music).

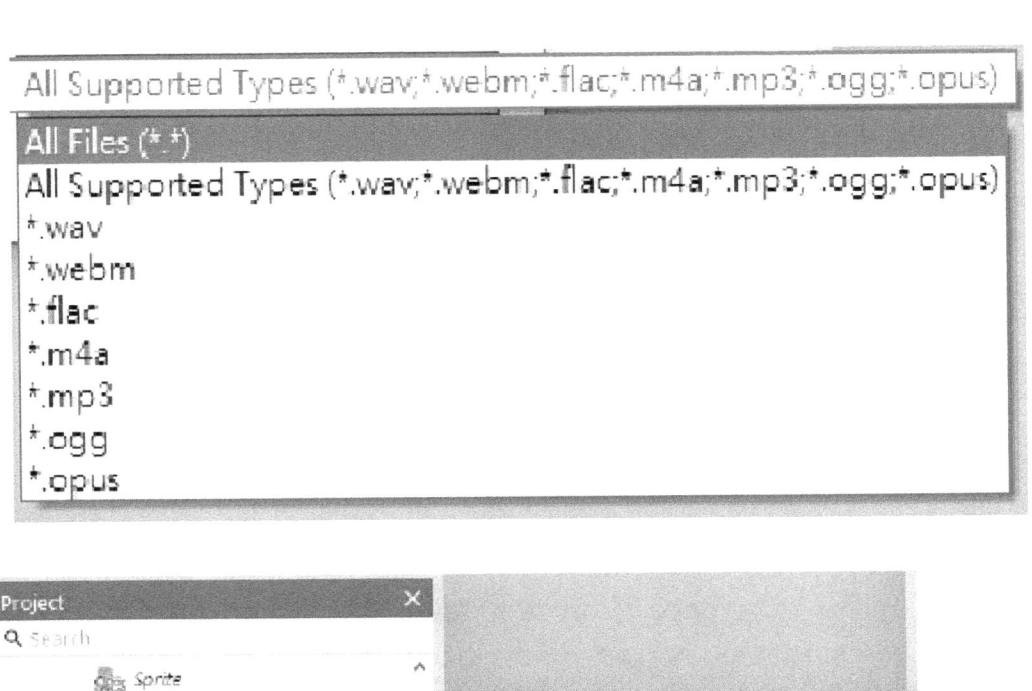

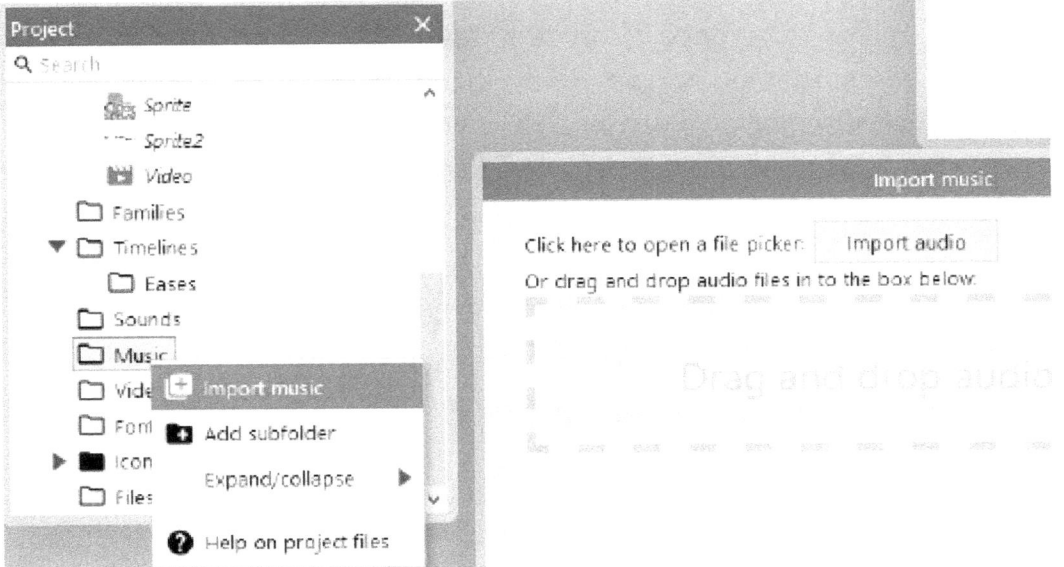

What types of 3D game can be created with Construct 3?

It appears that C3 is now capable of doing 3D. When a game is truly 3D, game objects are polygonal and there is at least one 3D camera view.

3D games are polygonal because polygons, particularly triangles, are the simplest shapes that can efficiently represent complex 3D objects in a virtual space. Triangles are the fundamental building blocks in 3D graphics because they are always flat and simple to process. Any 3D shape can be approximated by dividing it into smaller triangles (a process called "tessellation"). Graphics hardware (like GPUs) is optimized to handle triangles very efficiently. This allows for real-time rendering of complex scenes and animations.

While triangles are the base, multiple triangles can combine to create more complex shapes, from characters to environments. The more triangles, the smoother and more detailed an object looks. Using polygons allows game developers to strike a balance between visual detail and performance. Fewer polygons mean a game runs faster, while more polygons increase visual fidelity at the cost of performance. Polygons also work well with textures (2D images wrapped around 3D models). Since triangles are flat, mapping a texture onto them is straightforward, which helps in creating realistic-looking surfaces.

Different camera views provide unique perspectives, affecting how a game is played:
* First-person view (FPV) immerses players directly into the game world, as if they are seeing through the eyes of the character. This is common in shooter games because it increases realism and personal connection.
* Third-person view (TPV) shows the character from behind or from a distance, allowing players to see the surroundings more broadly. It's useful in action-adventure and platformer games for better spatial awareness.
* Top-down or isometric views offer a god-like perspective and are often used in strategy or role-playing games where players need to control multiple characters or manage resources.

Different camera views can be used to create specific emotional responses. First-person views create intimacy and immersion, making players feel more connected to the character's emotions. Cinematic cameras, on the other hand, help tell the story by framing scenes dramatically, like in movies.

Perspective 3D:

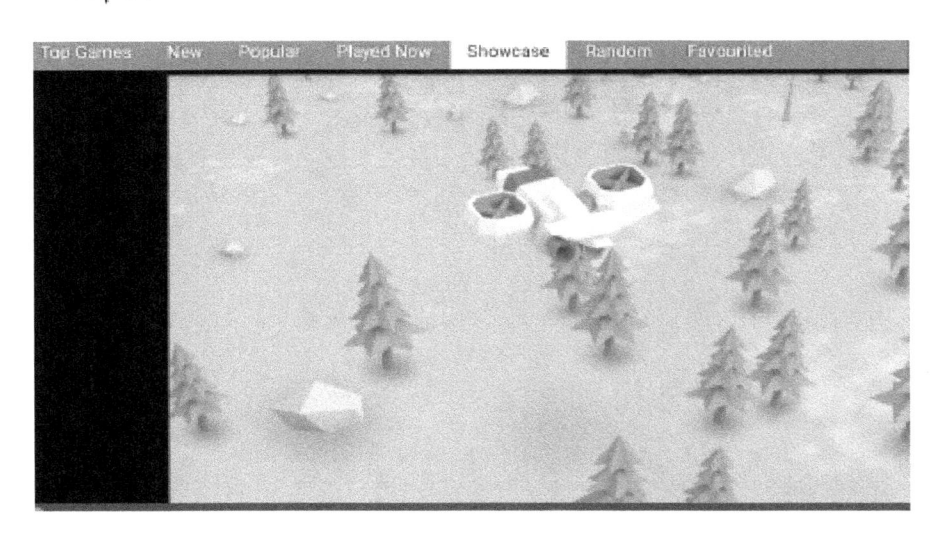

Simple polygonal:

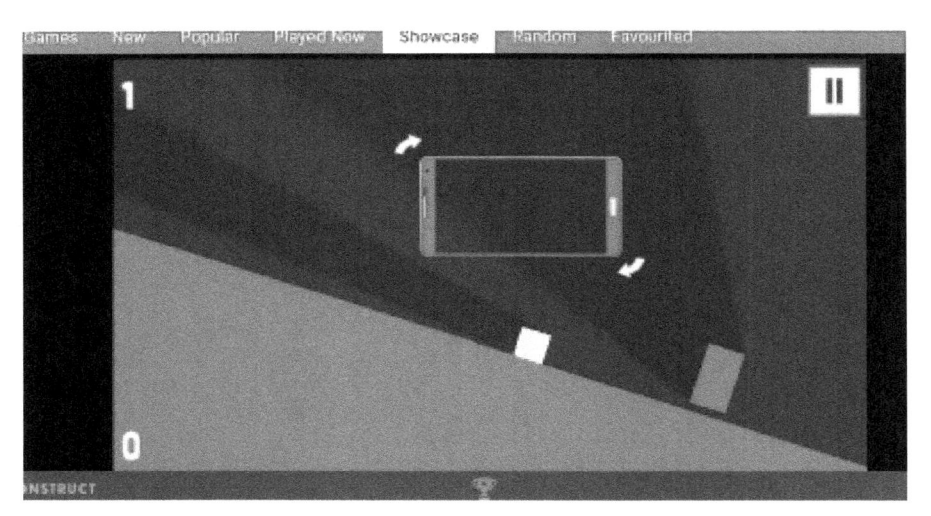

Top-down shooter:

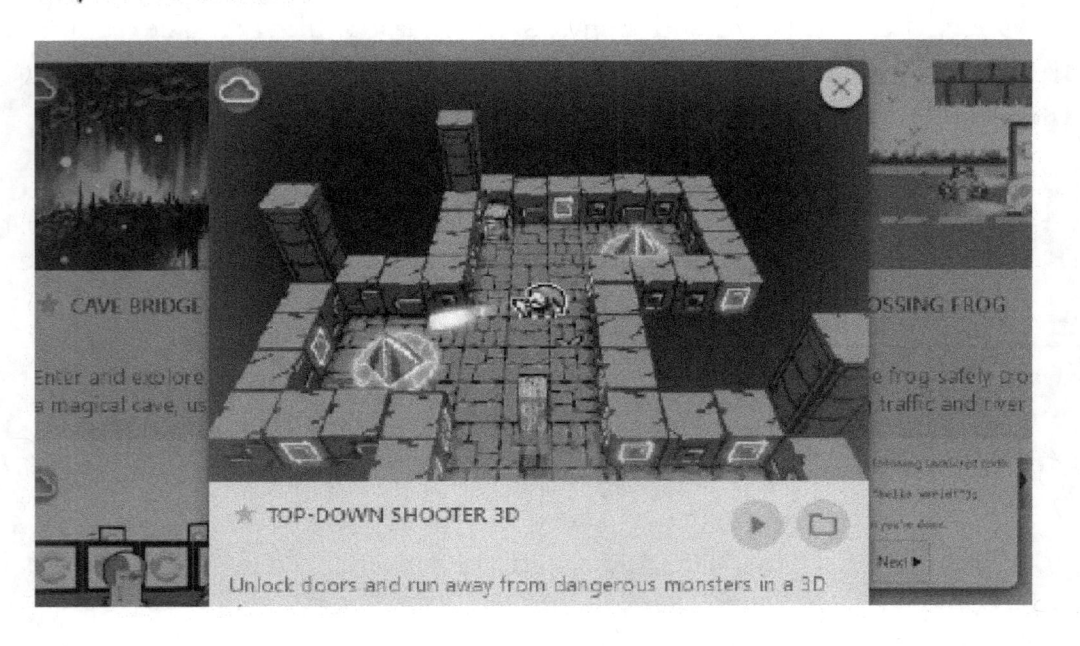

3D racer:

3D Bird Eye View:

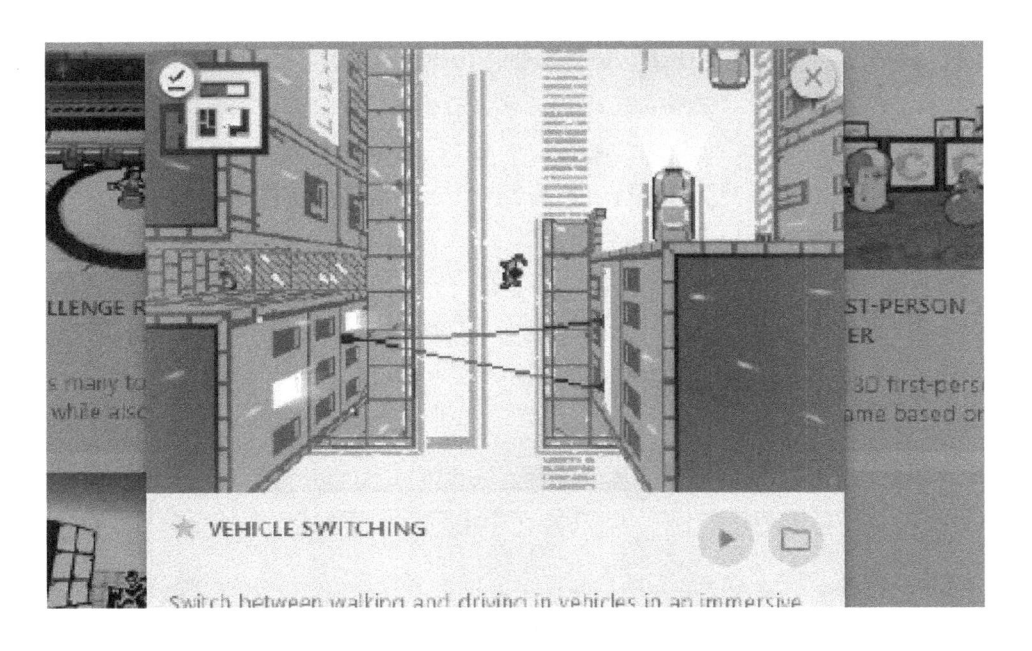

FPS shooter:

What Construct 3 features can be used to produce 3D games?

Construct 3 introduced the 3D Shape plugin, which allows users to create basic 3D shapes such as Cubes, Pyramids, Prisms, and Cylinders. These shapes can be manipulated in 3D space by adjusting properties like size, position, rotation, and texture. Developers can apply 2D textures to these 3D shapes to create simple objects with depth.

The 3D Camera system in Construct 3 allows developers to adjust the perspective of the scene in 3D space. Key features of the camera include:

- Rotation and movement in the X, Y, and Z axes.
- Field of view (FOV) adjustments, giving control over the camera's perspective.
- Position and orientation of the camera to look at objects from different angles.

This feature enables more dynamic viewpoints and adds depth to traditionally 2D games by integrating 3D-like camera control.

Construct 3 also introduces the concept of Z elevation, where sprites and other 2D elements can be moved along the Z-axis, creating the illusion of depth. This allows objects to appear closer or farther away, simulating a 3D space without using actual 3D models.

Construct 3 also offers various shader effects that simulate depth and 3D visuals, such as:

- Perspective distortion: This effect warps 2D objects to give them a more 3D-like appearance when viewed from different angles.
- Depth of field: Developers can simulate a sense of depth by making objects in the distance appear blurred while those in the foreground remain sharp.

What Construct 3 3D feature has been used in the Vehicle Switching template (aka 3D City)?

Z elevation has been used in the code right from the start. The screenshot below is kinda self-explanatory.

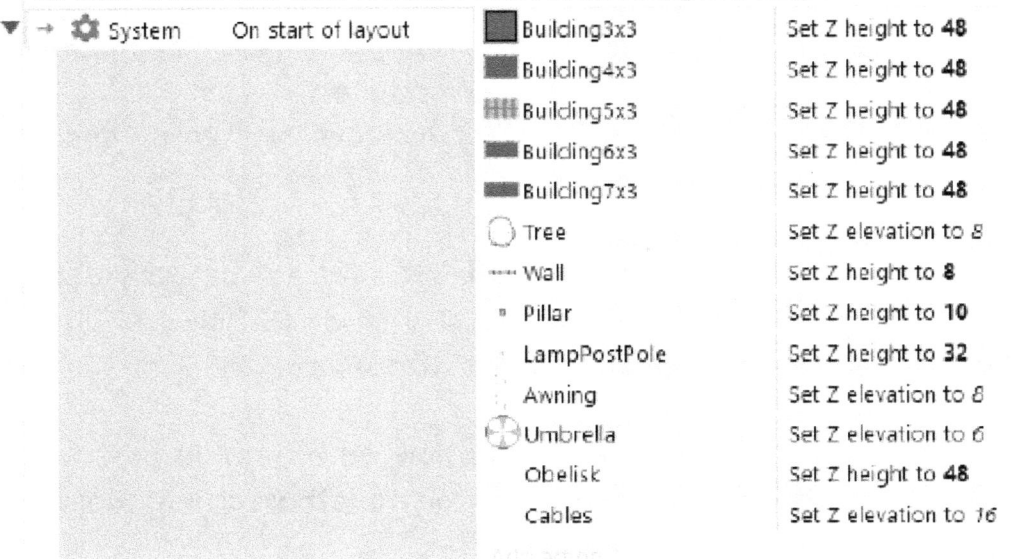

The Z Elevation property determines how far an object is positioned along the Z-axis (depth axis) relative to the 2D layout. By changing it you can make an object appear to be "above" or "below" other objects in the scene. It's as if you're moving the object closer to or farther away from the camera.

- When you increase the Z Elevation of an object, it appears to rise up or move forward into the scene, away from the background.
- When you decrease the Z Elevation, the object appears to sink or move back into the scene, closer to the background.

Do note that Z Elevation only affects the visual positioning of an object. It does not influence collision detection or interaction with other objects. These are still handled based on the 2D coordinates. Also, Z Elevation interacts with the 3D Camera, allowing objects to visually move toward or away from the camera in 3D space.

Z Height controls how tall an object is along the Z-axis, effectively determining the thickness or vertical dimension of an object. Adjusting it can give objects an additional sense of 3D volume, making them appear taller or thicker in the 3D space.

- When you increase the Z Height of an object, it appears to extend upward, giving the impression that the object is thicker or taller.
- When you decrease the Z Height, the object appears flatter or shorter along the Z-axis.

Note that it is primarily a visual property as well - it does not directly affect how an object interacts with other objects, but it influences how the object looks when viewed from different angles using the 3D camera.

Simply put, Z Elevation determines how high or low an object is positioned in 3D space, while Z Height controls how thick or tall that object appears along the Z-axis.

Z elevation has been used in the On-rails Shooter template:

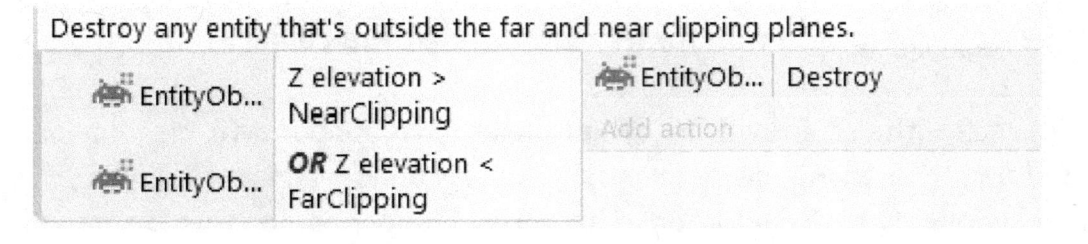

You can also change the Z elevation of entire layers so to move all the objects on the layer up and down on the Z axis.

What Construct 3 3D feature has been used in the First Person Shooter template?

It is the 3D Camera that has been used here to give a 2D game a 3D style display view:

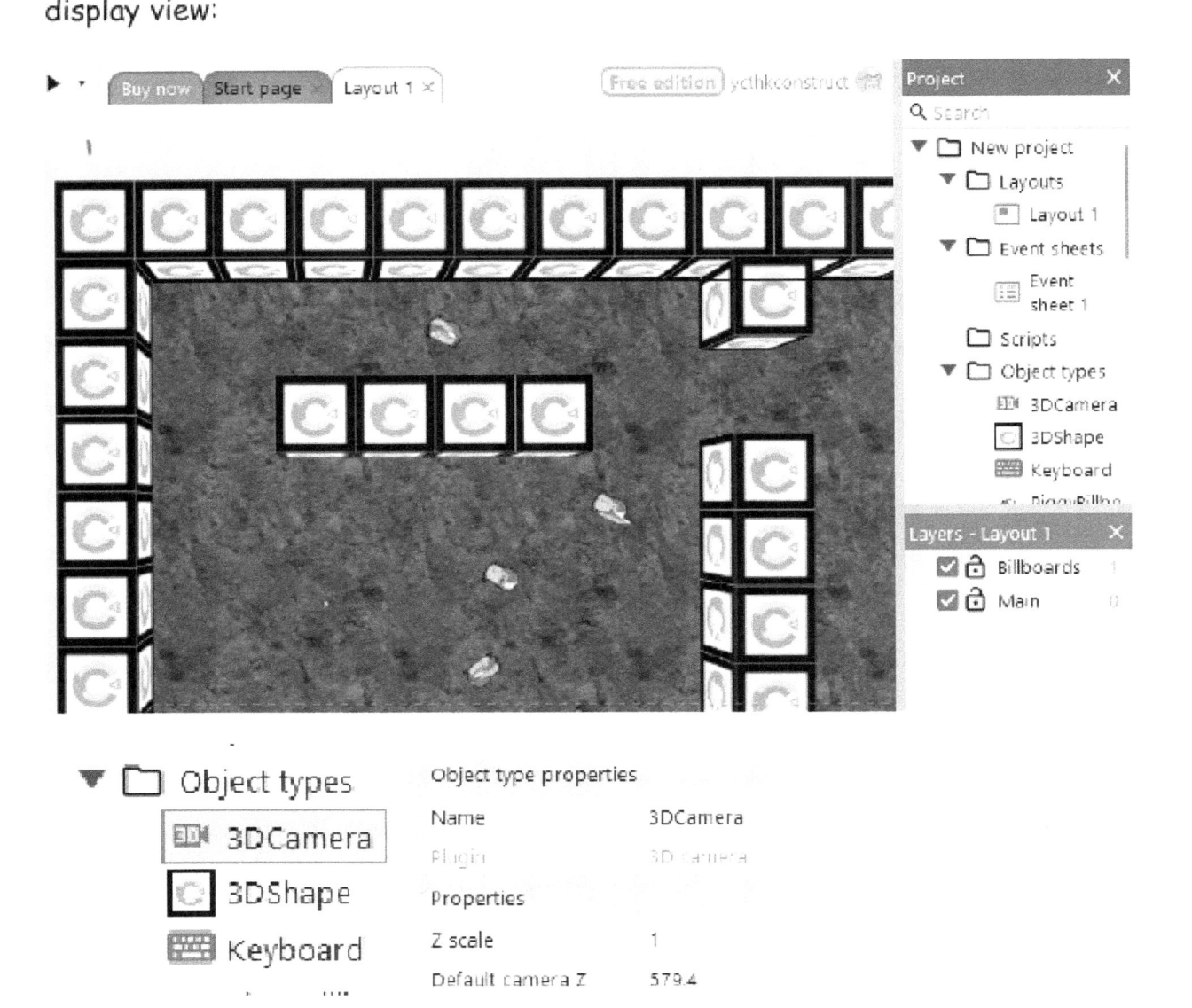

You can see the 3D Camera object in the list of objects. Note that it will only apply to layers which have the Rendering mode property set to 3D. Layers with a 2D rendering mode will simply ignore the 3D Camera altogether.

Look at position is what sets the position and orientation of the 3D Camera. Note that the look-at positions are given as 3D co-ordinates. Look parallel to layout is also relevant as it can set the position and orientation of the 3D Camera using a camera position and a camera angle in degrees. It effectively sets a camera position looking along the layout in such a way that the layout appears as the floor at the bottom of the screen.

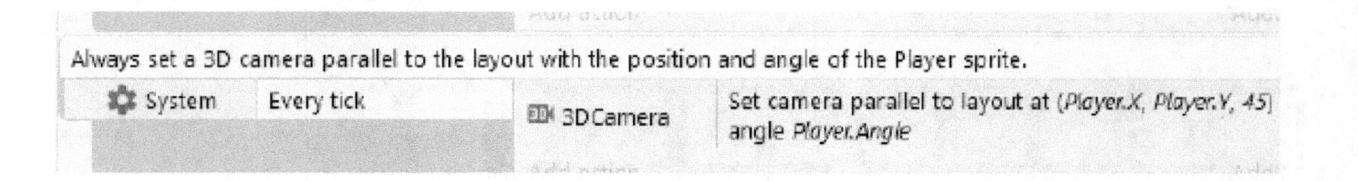

Always set a 3D camera parallel to the layout with the position and angle of the Player sprite.			
⚙ System	Every tick	3D Camera	Set camera parallel to layout at (*Player.X*, *Player.Y*, *45*) angle *Player.Angle*

The 3D shape object is simply a basic element that can be used to add 3D to a project. On a 3D box you can have 6 images drawn to cover each face of the shape (via set face image). You can also set its Z height via set Z height.

www.gameengines.net

Please email your questions and comments to editor@HobbyPRESS.net.